Multicore Computer Architectures

Patrick H. Stakem

© 2013

4th edition, 2016

Contents

Introduction

A Multicore computer architecture uses two or more (up to 100's) of cpu's, configured into a multiprocessor on a single chip. Each cpu can fetch and execute its own instructions, and has a method to communicate with the other cpu's. If an embedded chip has a cpu, memory, and I/O on a single chip, a multicore architecture has an entire network of parallel processors on a single chip. In the same sense that a computer used to fill a room, then was reduced to a box, then to a chip, we now see a further reduction of multiple cpu's. It's just Moore's law. Every 18 months or so, the technology can give us a 2x factor of improvement.

For the longest time, the state of the technology only allowed putting one cpu on a chip. As things progressed along the lines of Moore's Law, the separate floating point unit was incorporated onto the same chip. Then came cache memory. We are now at the point where we can put multiple cpu's on a chip; these are called cores.

Before they were all integrated onto the same piece of silicon, they could be glued together in a multichip module, a silicon circuit board arrangement.

Author

Mr. Stakem has an undergraduate degree in Electrical Engineering from Carnegie Mellon University, and

Master's in Computer Science and Physics from the Johns Hopkins University.

He taught for Loyola University in Maryland, the Johns Hopkins University, and Capitol Technology University. He spent 42 years supporting projects at all of the NASA Centers. He has a particular fascination with technology.

Mr. Stakem can be found on Facebook and Linkedin.

The Intergraph C4 Multichip Module

But just being able to cram more cpu's on a single piece of silicon doesn't solve out high- performance requirements problem. There are bottlenecks introduced in this approach, and they must be addressed. This lesson was learned many years ago with multiprocessors. The technology has changed, but the architectural limitations are the same.

Cover picture, Courtesy CPUShack.

Intel Pentium II

The limitations to computer performance tend to be either the instruction rate of the cpu itself, or the channel capacity of the various data paths involved. One approach to increased performance is parallelism.

Some performance enhancements come from the architecture of the multiprocessor. For example, interrupt processing can be offloaded to a non-busy cpu.

One issue is how interrupts are handled in multiprocessing. How are interrupts steered to the proper processor? It is a function of the operating system. In the same way that processes are assigned to certain processors, interrupts and their associated interrupt handling are also assigned. Binding interrupts to specific cpu's is not necessarily the proper approach; since this approach does not improve hits in cache memory Multiple interrupts can overload the selected processor. Handling interrupts is a task, and task allocation is a function of the operating system. A multiprocessing operating system is required to manage the unique issues of multiprocessor hardware.

Another issue is cache coherency. In multicore architectures, each CPU core has its own L1 cache, but share L2 caches with other cores. Local data in the L1 caches must be consistent with data in other L1 caches. If one core changes a value in cache due to a write operation, that data needs to be changed in other caches as well (if they hold the same item).

This problem is well known, and addressed by studies from the field of multiprocessing. The issues can be addressed by several mechanisms. In cache snooping, each cache monitors the others for changes. If a change in value is seen, the local cached copy is invalidated. This means it will have to be re-accessed from the next level before use. A global directory of cached data can also be maintained. Several protocols for cache coherency include MSI, MESI, and others.

A multicore processor has multiple cpu and memory elements in a single chip. Being on a single chip reduces the communications times between elements, and allows for multiprocessing. Advances in microelectronics fabrication techniques lead to the implementation of multi-cores for desktop and server machines around 2007. It was becoming increasingly difficult to increase clock speeds, so the obvious approach was to turn to parallelism. Currently, in this market, quad-core, 6-core, and 8-core chips are available. Besides additional cpu's, additional on-chip memory must be added, usually in the form of memory caches, to keep the processors fed with instructions and data. There is no inherent difference in multicore architectures and multiprocessing with single core chips, except in the speed of communications. The standard interconnect technologies used in multiprocessing and clustering are applied to inter-core communications.

We can compare multi-core devices to large parallel machines of some 10 years past, in the same sense that we can compare a single-chip cpu to large mainframe systems of 20-25 years ago. Things have gotten smaller and more capable at the same time. What used to fill a room went to a file cabinet size, then a desktop box size, then to a single chip.

Coupling between cores can be tight or loose. A tightly coupled system usually is implemented with shared memory. A loosely coupled system generally uses communication channels between cores.

CPU

To understand computers, we must understand how they operate. In this section, we will briefly review the elements of a computer, the fetch/execute cycle, and how instructions are executed.

Any computer can be thought of as having three main elements or building blocks. These are the Processing Element (PE), the Memory, and the Input/Output section. The processing element handles the mathematical and logical operations on data, and the flow of control. The memory, which is usually organized hierarchically, holds the data and instructions. The I/O section allows for the user interface, and provides a communication path to other systems or devices.

It is important to remember that processor and memory speeds are not always well matched, and processing time compared to I/O time is out of balance.

Memories are dense, regular silicon structures. Processors are dense, not very regular structures. Processors tend to be regular along the word size, but memories are millions of the same cell design, replicated to the limits of manufacturing technology. Memory production lends itself to economy of scale much more so than processors.

A processor element is a unit that performs operations on data. The form of the operations depends on the form of the data. Different types of PE's exist, for general purpose, floating point, vector, and multimedia data sets.
This section discusses how an instruction gets executed. The basic process is referred to as the *fetch/execute cycle*. First the instruction is fetched from memory, and then the instruction is executed, which can involve the fetching and writing of data items. Some units, like FPU's generally do not fetch their own instructions; this is done for them by the integer ALU. The FPU acts as a co-processor, tightly coupled to its ALU.

Instructions are executed in steps called *machine cycles*. Each machine cycle might take several machine clock times to complete. If the architecture is pipelined, then each machine cycle consists of a stage in the pipeline. At each step, a memory access or an internal operation (ALU operation) is performed. Machine cycles are sequenced by a state machine in the CPU logic, driven by a clock source.

A register called the *program counter* (pc) contains the location in memory of the next instruction to be executed. The contents of the program counter get automatically updated as the instruction executes. The address of the next instruction to be executed (not necessarily the next adjacent instruction) is put in the program counter. A *register* is a temporary holding memory for data, and is part of the CPU. At initialization time (boot), the program counter is loaded with the location of the first instruction to be executed. After that, it is simply incremented, unless there is a change in the flow of control, such as a branch or jump. In this case, the target address of the branch or jump is put into the program counter.

The first step of the instruction execution is to fetch the instruction from memory into a special holding location called the *Instruction Register*. At this point, the instruction is decoded, meaning a control unit figures out, from the bit pattern, what the instruction is to do. This control unit implements the *ISA*, the instruction set architecture. Without getting too complicated, we could have a flexible control unit that could execute different ISA's. That's possible, but beyond the scope of our discussion here.

With the instruction decode complete, the machine knows what resources are required for instruction execution. A typical math instruction, for example, would require two data reads from memory, an Arithmetic Logic Unit (ALU) operation, and a data write. The data items might be in registers, or memory.

The ISA for a processor defines its basic machine language instructions. Each machine language instruction maps into one or more micro-instructions in the control unit. The software view of the CPU is the ISA. If we want to program the CPU, we write a series of machine code instructions.

ALU

The arithmetic-logic unit performs arithmetic and logical operations on integer data. The integers can be from 2 bits to 64 bits in length, actually, any size we want. The arithmetic operations are add, subtract, multiply, and divide. The logical operations are AND, OR, NEGATE, Exclusive-OR (XOR), and some variations on these.

The ALU is also generally used for flow of control, keeping and updating a program counter to make sure the instructions are executed in the right order. If we encounter a data-dependent branch, the results have to be calculated, and the proper path of the branch taken. If a subroutine is called, we go off from the mainstream of the program, and need to get back when the subroutine is done. External hardware may trigger an interrupt, and the mechanics of handling this looks like a subroutine call.

FPU

The floating point unit performs arithmetic operations on floating point data. The floating point format resembles scientific or engineering notation, consisting of an integer mantissa, and an integer exponent of 2. Floating point numbers have greater dynamic range than integers, but do not necessarily hold an accurate representation. Floating point units can sometimes perform arithmetic operations on large (128-bit) integer data. Floating point units are usually an adjunct to an ALU, and do not generally fetch their own instructions. Floating point software running on an integer ALU was originally used, but was very slow.

DSP

A Digital Signal Processor (DSP) is similar to a general purpose CPU, but provides specialized operations for DSP-type operations on specialized data formats. Originally, the DSP function would be implemented by software running in a general purpose CPU. DSP operations usually have time deadline constraints (hard real time requirements), and the throughput of the CPU is limited. DSP for audio evolved from sonar processing, and video data processing evolved from radar.

DSP's operate on multimedia data types, and include special-purpose operations derived from the digital signal processing realm. This includes the Multiply-and-Accumulate (mac), a digital filtering primitive. DSP's can be implemented in Multicore variants.

GPU

The graphics processing unit performs arithmetic operations on image data. These were introduced in the late 1990's as specialized architectures optimized for processing of large blocks of graphics data in parallel. Their instruction set is targeted to operations performed on 3D graphics data, such as transformations and rendering. Although these were originally targeted to computer gaming applications, it was not lost on scientists and engineers that this was the type of matrix manipulation and digital filtering that they employed in many different areas. The GPU is not general-purpose, but is targeted and optimized to operate on matrix data structures. GPU's are now used for many general-purpose scientific and engineering computing across a range of platforms. The term GPU was invented by high-performance graphics vendor nVidia.

Using high-level languages, GPU-accelerated applications can run the sequential part of the workload on a CPU, optimized for single-threaded performance, while running parallel processing on the GPU. This is referred to as "GPU computing."

GPU-computing is possible because today's GPU does a lot more than just render graphics: It might achieve a teraflop of floating point performance.

The first GPU's were designed as graphics accelerators, supporting only specific fixed-function pipelines. Starting in the late 1990s, the hardware became increasingly programmable. Less than a year after the GPU first appeared, it was being applied in various technical computing fields because of its excellent floating point performance. The General Purpose GPU, GPGPU as nVidia calls it, had appeared. Derived from that, we get GPU computing.

Initially, GPU's ran graphics programming languages such as OpenGL. Developers had to map scientific calculations onto problems that could be represented by triangles and polygons. A breakthrough came when a group of Stanford University researchers set out to re-purpose the GPU as a "streaming processor."

In 2003, Brook was introduced as the first widely adopted programming model to extend C with data-parallel constructs. Using concepts such as streams, kernels and reduction operators, the Brook compiler and runtime system presented the GPU as a general-purpose processor in a high-level language. Most importantly, Brook programs were not only easier to write than hand-tuned GPU code, they were many times faster. GPU's process high speed video data on phones, tablets, and tv's, and also find wide application in scientific and financial computing.

TFU

Texture filtering units (TFU's) are specialized processors which are used to rotate and resize a two dimensional bitmap. This involves a large matrix multiply in 3-dimensional space. This function can be done in a CPU, but the TFU is highly optimized for this task. These units evolved from computer-based gaming, but are highly applicable to scientific and financial data visualization.

Getting to the core

These units just discussed perform the operations, but are just a part of the computer. We also need local storage in the cpu, and these are called the registers. We need a way to address and access memory. We need to be able to handle interrupts and direct memory access operations. We need virtual memory support.

A cpu chip will have all of this functionality on it. If there is a fpu, the integer cpu will handle the addressing, the decoding of instructions, the I/O and such. Within the CPU, we can have localized parallelism, such as multiple instruction dispatch units, multiple pipelines, and multiple ALU's. But a lot of the circuitry is in common.

In a cpu, we would expect to find modern optimization features to keep the various arithmetic units working full time. The techniques of Instruction Level Parallelism (ILP) are applied, initially by the compiler, but also by the hardware during execution of instructions. Common hardware approaches within a cpu could include superpipelining, superscalar, speculative execution, and many others. We would expect to see these in each core of a multi-core device. There is a limit to how effective all this is, referred to as the Instruction Level parallelism (ILP) wall.

A thread of execution is the smallest set of associated code managed by the cpu. Threads compete with each other for processor resources such as the instruction execution pipeline and the data and instructions in cache. Threads are managed by the Operating System.

In multicore, each core incorporates the functionality of a cpu – it fetches and executes its own instructions, it handles its own interrupts and memory fetches. Inside the core, multiple pipelines and ALU's/FPU may be implemented.

Multiprocessor

Multiprocessing allows us to apply the resources of multiple cpu's and their associated memory's to a single problem. If one cpu is fast, aren't more faster? Maybe.

Multiprocessing can be implemented as the execution of multiple concurrent processes, under the control of an operating system. It is not time-sharing or multitasking. Multiprocessors have, by definition, more than one processor.

Flynn's Taxonomy recognizes four classes of computing machines. These are single instruction-single data (SISD), like a single cpu, single instruction-multiple data (SIMD); multiple instruction-single data, and multiple instruction-multiple data. Multiprocessors are MIMD. SIMD machines execute the same sequence of instructions or thread on different data sets, as might be the case in vector processing. MISD is not seen much, but can be used to implement redundant computing.

MIMD does have challenges in the areas of resource contention, and the possibility of deadlock. Threads may contend for resources in a complex way that is difficult to manage globally. The Operating system is supposed to handle this. Semaphores are used to manage contention, much like in real-time operating systems.

The bottleneck to getting more than one processor to work on a given problem domain at one time is the communications. There is an upper bound in a bus-oriented, shared memory SMP systems, arising from the communication limit of the bus interconnect (a classic Shannon channel limit). Clusters of computers also suffer from an inter-processor communication limit, from the LAN-like interconnect. Some MPP's are like clusters in a box.

All processors are the same in a symmetric multiprocessor. We can have different processor types, in which case it is referred to as asymmetric. In core terms, we can have an asymmetric configuration with a cpu and a DSP.

Coupling between processors can be tight or loose. Tightly coupled systems are connected by a bus, and use shared memory. A multi-core architecture is a chip level multiprocessor. Tightly coupled systems have better performance, and have greater energy efficiency. Networks connect loosely coupled multiprocessors. A Cluster computer is an example.

Shared-memory MPP's usually do not have a homogeneous communication environment, due to communication bandwidth restrictions. A two tier communications architecture is used, with shared memory intrabox, and a lan-type point-point link for interbox messaging. Since MPP machines have to scale to thousands of processors, a distributed memory scheme is usually chosen. Another approach is to cluster SMP's. Data sharing is the key, and the critical issue for large parallel relational database applications. The performance will be made (or broken) by the sophistication of the interconnection scheme. Speed and latency are of critical importance. Latency predominates for short messages.

Consider the case of having to send a large volume of data from New York to California. We look at two options: we rent a gigabit class line, and transfer the data serially at OC-48, or about 2.4 gigabits per second. The latency, from the time a bit enters the line at New York until it exits at California, is very short, and depends on the time it takes light to traverse 2000 miles of cable. This is an expensive option. We could also decide to charter a 747 freighter, and load it with floppy disks. Here, the latency is about 5 hours, but the data all arrives together. One case emphasizes speed, the other case emphasizes low latency.

Again, let's look at an analogy. If we want to get across town using the bus system, we wait at the bus stop for the next available bus. The wait time is our latency, and is random, depending on when we arrive with respect to the bus's arrival. If we go only a few blocks, the latency may be commensurate with or even exceed the travel time. If we go across country on the bus, the latency is totally dominated by the travel time. Even in town, if we need to change buses, we introduce another latency between getting dropped off by bus-1 and picked up by bus-2. We may need to cross town in several of these 'hops', each with its own latency. For one person, this may not be efficient. For large aggregates of people, it makes sense.

Alternately, we can call a cab, and go directly from where we are to our destination. There is still a wait-latency, but the travel time is reduced, and the cost is higher. The best case, the fastest travel time, is that we jump into a worm-hole that connects directly where we want to go. Then, the hole closes up behind us.

In the interconnect hierarchy, the node-node connection is frequently made via shared memory. Thus, a node may be an SMP architecture in its own right, with two or four processor elements. this approach does not scale well beyond about 16 processors. The node-node communication is tightly coupled.

Between nodes, a loosely coupled message passing scheme is usually employed. This uses a LAN-like architecture that can take one of many topological forms. Popular are the mesh, torus, hypercube, and tree.

Any given data processing architecture will have bottlenecks, because either the processor is waiting for the memory (processor stall), or the memory is waiting for the processor (I/O bound). Communications speed is limited by the minimum channel capacity in the system, and processing speed is limited by the slowest hardware element. Ideally, the computation rate should balance the I/O rate, but this is a function of the problem domain, and the algorithm. Some data can be buffered in memory, but on-chip memory is an expensive resource.

For example, the combination of four serial links of one Transputer together can transmit a total of about 1 million 32 bit words per second, both in and out simultaneously. If the on-chip ram is used primarily for instructions, and most data is flowed through the data links, then for each new word of data, 10 instructions can be executed. The on-chip 4k can hold a significant amount of code for the RISC Architecture and the data links can in theory supply new data fast enough for even the shortest algorithms and tightest loops. In other words, the data handling and computational speeds seem to be well matched. The data can be supplied by either the results of prior processes or by transputers used for data routing . The data routers will each have expanded external memories and can be thought of as servers for large blocks of shared data. The data routers will serve as very smart gate keepers of that data for the main processing engine. They can also be used as system masters to hold and execute large blocks of less time critical code for high level control of computational resources. They might even swap time critical code in and out of the main engine in real time as tasks change.

If 10% of the code consumes 90% of the time which is a commonly assumed ratio, then a well balanced system would consist of multiple Transputers to run time critical code with data routers able to support caching of less frequently used code, to control system overall dataflow, and to provide redundancy.

Looking at how a typical executing program might be balanced in this system, assume five identical processes being executed in parallel. Data routing Transputers send a 32 bit data word to one instrument Transputer. These instrument transputers execute 10 instructions then pass a 32 bit result on to another instrument Transputer which execute 10 instructions and so on down a string of 20 Transputers (200 instructions executed total) and the result is sent back to the data routers. So long as at least 200 instructions need to be executed for each new word of data, the instrument transputers are not starved for data. Clearly, this is an idealized example and no parallel processor can be 100% efficient in using instruction cycles. The point is that this architecture is within the range of a reasonable data-flow-to-processing ratio.

Scalable systems, those made up of multiple computational & communication building blocks, have an architecture that is responsive to the problem domain. In such a homogeneous system, the correct amount of processing and I/O can be provided for the initial requirements, with the ability to expand later in a building block fashion to address evolved requirements as well as redundancy or fault tolerance. Developing software for scalable systems is a challenge, mostly in deciding how the software is spread across the computational nodes. This is a solvable problem, based both on good software tools and on programmer experience. Research into these topics as well as the ability of the system itself to adapt to processing load, is ongoing. Transputer networks, discussed in chapter seven, use modular building blocks with integral communication capabilities to build networks that can offer linear problem speedup. This is obvious with compute-intensive, minimal communication tasks such as the Mandelbrot set, which could ideally use one processor element per pixel to calculate the image. Each point in the Mandelbrot set is independent of its neighbors. If we run a particular instance of the Mandelbrot set on a single Transputer, then multiple units, and graph the run times against the number of processor elements, we will see a near-linear speedup. In the general case this is true, until the problem becomes more communication bound than compute bound. As a "best case", the Mandelbrot is an ideal benchmark; completely computationally intensive.

Of course, the applicability of the parallel processor to a given problem set implies that the applicable algorithm can be parallelized, and a solution can be implemented and debugged in a reasonable time. This implies that an efficient programming and debugging environment exist for the selected hardware. This is certainly the case for Transputer-based systems. The major hurdle is conceptual for the systems integrators - the ability to think in parallel paradigms. This comes with hands-on experience. Multicore is multiprocessing in one package.

InterProcessor Communication

In this section, we address different architectural approaches to coordinating the use of multiple processors. Most of these approaches will work with any underlying technology, and are useful after the maximum speed of a single processor in a given technology has been wrung out; ie, we are implementing a multiprocessor.

One approach to solving increasing complex problems with increasingly capable hardware is simply to wait. Given enough time, sufficiently complex hardware for the problem domain will emerge. However, it is increasingly apparent that software development lags hardware to the extent that software tools do not emerge until the hardware is obsolete by at least two generations. Also, the capabilities of any given hardware design will be exceeded by computational problems of interest well into the foreseeable future. At any given point of technological complexity, a cluster of coordinated processors can outperform a single processor. Thus, faced with a seemingly inexhaustible complex problem domain, along with industry emphasis on hardware development, we need to tackle both the software and the communication domains to better utilize the hardware available at any given point. Software will be discussed later. Here, we want to discuss the critical issue of communications among elements.

The bottleneck to getting more than one processor to work on a given problem domain at one time is the communications. There is an upper bound in a bus-oriented, shared memory SMP systems, arising from the communication limit of the bus interconnect (a classic Shannon communication channel limit). Clusters of computers also suffer from an inter-processor communication limit, from the LAN-like interconnect. Some MPP's are like clusters in a box. Multicore now gives us a cluster on a chip.

Shared memory MPP's usually do not have a homogeneous communication environment, due to communication bandwidth restrictions. A two tier communications architecture is used, with shared memory intrabox, and a lan type point-point link for interbox messaging. Since MPP machines have to scale to thousands of processors, a distributed memory scheme is usually chosen. Another approach is to cluster SMP's. Data sharing is the key, and the critical issue for large parallel relational database applications. The performance will be made (or broken) by the sophistication of the interconnection scheme. Speed and latency are of critical importance. Latency predominates for short messages

Consider the case of having to send a large volume of data from New York to California. We look at two options: we rent a gigabit class line, and transfer the data serially at OC-48, or about 2.4 gigabits per second. The latency, from the time a bit enters the line at New York until it exits at California, is very short, and depends on the time it takes light to traverse 2000 miles of cable. This is an expensive option. We could also decide to charter a 747 freighter, and load it with DVD's. Here, the latency is about 5 hours, but the data all arrives together. One case emphasizes speed, the other case emphasizes low latency.

Again, lets look at an analogy. If we want to get across town using the bus system, we wait at the bus stop for the next available bus. The wait time is our latency, and is random, depending on when we arrive with respect to the bus's arrival. If we go only a few blocks, the latency may be commensurate with or even exceed the travel time. If we go across country on the bus, the latency is totally dominated by the travel time. Even in town, if we need to change buses, we introduce another latency between getting dropped off by bus-1 and picked up by bus-2. We may need to cross town in several of these 'hops', each with its own latency. For one person, this may not be efficient. For large aggregates of people, it makes sense.

Alternately, we can call a cab, and go directly from where we are to our destination. There is still a wait-latency, but the travel time is reduced, but the cost is higher.

In the interconnect hierarchy, the node-node connection can be made via shared memory. A node may be an SMP architecture in its own right, with two or four processor elements. this approach does not scale well beyond about 16 processors. The node-node communication is tightly coupled.

Between nodes, a loosely coupled message passing scheme is usually employed. This uses a LAN-like architecture, which can take one of many topological forms. Popular are the mesh, torus, hypercube, and tree. The following table shows the approaches taken by some of the major vendors. Each of these interconnect approaches will be examined in the subsequent sections.

The Mesh

The mesh is an n-dimensional grid, with processors at the vertices of the grid. If we assume that communications delay is linear in distance, then the mesh topology is very efficient. 'Distance' is the metric that expresses the communication cost between nodes.

The mesh architecture was favored by Intel for their Paragon series, based on work done at CalTech. The chip instantiation was called the iMRC (mesh router component). This allowed vendors to interconnect different chips such as the i860 and Pentium.

The early iPSC series used as many as one-hundred twenty-eight i860 chips. Special I/O nodes used a shared I/O design were based on the i80386. The internal networked, called 'Direct-Connect', provided bi-directional 5.6 Mbyte/second channels in a switched configuration. The Paragon machine scaled to 1024 of the i860 processors, arranged in SMP type, 4-processor nodes. Each node could have up to 128 Mbytes of memory. The interprocessor communication architecture scaled as nodes are added. A 2-D mesh configuration, with a mesh router for each node, provided a message passing architecture with a bi-directional node-node bandwidth of 200 Mbytes per second, and a latency of 40 Nanoseconds per node hop. Intel's Paragon machine scaled to 1024 of the 50 Mhz. i860 processors, arranged in SMP-type, 4 processor nodes. Each node could have up to 128 mbytes of memory. The nodes were interconnected in a mesh.

The Hypercube

The hypercube is an efficient topology for interconnection, because it provides a large number of interconnects, while keeping the maximum distance between any two nodes small. The number of nodes is restricted to a power of two, although incomplete hypercubes are possible. Each apex of the n-dimensional cube is a node. This allows a direct connection to each nearest neighbor in n-space. The hypercube is a good trade-off between maximum distance between nodes, and number of physical connections.

The hypercube architecture was used by nCube, the Intel iWarp, and the Transputer. In each case, the basic processor chip has a communications capability built in. The Transputer and the iWarp had 4 high speed serial nodes each, and the nCube chip had 12, going to 16 for the nCube3. Thus, the Transputer and iWarp can each be directly connected in an Order-4 hypercube, and the nCube2 in an order 12.

The iWarp achieved a communication to computation ratio of 1:1. Each iWarp component consisted of an integer and a floating point computation section, and a communication element. The communication element supported 4 full duplex I/O channels of 160 Mbytes/second input and output capability. Message passing exploited worm-hole routing for low overhead.

Multiple logical connections on one physical channel were possible, similar to Inmos' virtual link concept. Fine grained, systolic communication was supported.

A crossbar switch can be used if the processor does not support sufficient interconnects. The Inmos C004 16x16 crossbar switch chip provided this function for the serial links of the Transputer. A crossbar switch functions like a telephone company central office, connecting any input to any output upon demand. The circuit remains for the duration of the message, or can be quasi-permanent. The latency introduced by the switch is minimal, about 1/2 bit time in the Inmos case. This is important where several switches must be traversed by a message.

The nCube' machine's interconnection was via a hypercube topology. Each nCube2 had 13 I/O engines, one of which was used for external I/O. Thus, an order 12 Hypercube was supported, or up to 4096 nodes. The worst case (longest distance) communication latency is on the order of the Hypercube, or 12, in the case of the nCube machine. The nCube3 machine used a newer chip that operated at 50 Mhz. Up to 65k processors could be included, and each processor chip included 18 channels, 16 for the hypercube, and 2 for external I/O. The channels operated at 100mbps, due to use of 2 bit parallel (up from 1 bit, serial). nCubes's differentiater was its interconnection speed, at 2.5 megabytes/second bi-directional. The nCube-III had dynamic routing, where each channel supported transfers at 20 Mbytes/second. There were 18 communications channels on-chip, each 4 bits wide (2 in, 2 out). The channels operated at 2x clock, 50 mbytes/second peak each, or 200 mbytes/second aggregate. The latency was be less than 2 microseconds, with 200 nanosecond internode forwarding. Adaptive routing was used.

Another interconnect scheme is the tree structure. One variation of the tree architecture is the Fat Tree interconnect, which was favored by MPP maker Meiko and by Thinking Machines for the CM-5 series. A key factor is whether the tree is 'pruned' or complete. The maximum delay thru a tree architecture is on the order of the tree. Meiko's bisectional bandwidth scaled to 102 Gbytes/second. There was an independent low bandwidth parallel bus for diagnostics and maintenance.

The inter-processor communications topology and chips were of Meiko's design. The Elan and ELITE chip were produced by Texas Instruments. The ELAN was the network interface processor on each compute node. It provides a coherent Mbus processor interface. The ELITE was the network switch processor, a 4x4 full crossbar. The ELITE achieved a 10 microsecond latency with a linear (scalable) bisection bandwidth. What differentiated the CS-2 from the TMC CM-5 is that the

CS-2 used a complete tree interconnect, where the CM-5 used a pruned tree. In theory, the CS-2 had a larger bisectional bandwidth as the system scaled to larger numbers of nodes. The Meiko architecture supported up to eight layers in the tree, giving a worst case path in a 256 node configuration of 7 switches.

Each I/O connection of TMC's fat-tree interconnect provided a 20 Mbyte/second bisection bandwidth, that scaled. Latency ranged from 3-7 microseconds. The TM-5 machine was scalable to 16,000 units.

The Torus arrangement is a 3-D structure, used by early MPP vendors Tandem, Convex, and Cray's T3D. The T3D was scalable to hundreds or thousands of processors, using its sophisticated interconnect and memory system. It could support up to 2048 compute nodes, using a 3-D torus interconnection. The interconnect was bi-directional, 2 bytes wide, and gave a peak transfer rate of 300 Mbps between nodes. The sustained bandwidth was about half that. Transfers were directed, and packet switched. The T3D implemented Cray's shared distributed memory scheme, in which any processor can address any memory in the system.

The Convex MPP Exemplar supported up to 128 processors, organized as hype-nodes of up to 8 processors connected by a crossbar, of bandwidth 2.5

gigabytes/second. Interconnect latency was on the order of 100's of nanoseconds. Each hypernode had its own memory, which was shared among the processors in the hypernode. A hypernode can be thought of as a tightly coupled, shared memory SMP. I/O interfaces were distributed across the hypernodes. A second level torroidal interconnect was used between hypernodes. This scalable torroidal interconnect was based on the IEEE Scalable Coherent Interface (IEEE 1596-1992), and provided 4 unidirectional rings with a capacity of up to 2 gigabytes per second. Sequential access to memory was interleaved across the rings of the toroid, for load balancing. The hypernode can be thought as a tightly coupled, fine-grained system, and the collection of hypernodes can be thought of as a coarse-grained, message-passing architecture. The overall machine had coherent distributed memory, and a large I/O system that was also distributed. Sixty-four channels per I/O unit could be used, to a total of 4096 channels. The Service processor functionality was distributed among the hypernodes, with options for boot, diagnostics, and monitoring. A systems console (service hypernode) was used, with a separate and independent DaRT (diagnostic and remote testing bus), that operated in parallel with the interconnect busses.

If the IPC is located inside the chip, we have multicore. If it is inside the box, we have a multiprocessor. If it involves connecting boxes, we have a cluster. These are loose definitions. The concepts of connecting the processing units with each other remain the same.

Reconfigurable topologies

A parallel program's efficiency depends on the communication topology. This means this factor must be considered by the programmer, and it makes the porting of code from a machine with one topology to another with a different topology very difficult. Topologys can be made configurable with cross-bar switches, or with virtual links.

Statically Reconfigurable Systems

In a statically reconfigurable system, the communications interconnect topology is pre-configured before run time for a schema that the systems analyst has selected. The communications system then remains in that format throughout the run. For example, the analyst could choose a ring, a torus, a hypercube, or a mesh.

Dynamically Reconfigurable Systems

In a dynamically reconfigurable system, the communications interconnect topology can be changed at run time. The implications of this are that, in case of error, you may not know the machine state, or the interconnect state. A much better set of debugging tools is needed for this class of machine.

The advantage of a dynamic reconfiguration capability is that it allows the machine itself to search for optimal communication topologies for given problem sets. This may take the form of searching in a solution space for the minimization of a particular cost function, usually associated with run time (time to solution). Metrics such as processor loading or communications link usage may be considered.

Shared memory

If we have 2 or 4 processors, we may connect these with a multiported memory. The memory would include the contention resolution mechanisms to arbitrate between processors attempting to access a single location simultaneously.

The problem with this approach is that multiported memory (MPM) is expensive, of small capacity, and does not scale well beyond about 4 ports. This approach, however, has some merit, particularly if the processors and MPM can be combined onto one chip, or multichip module.

Looking at the communication problem from another angle, we may decide to tackle it not from a memory but from an I/O standpoint. In the distributed memory approach, we have a processor and memory at each node, and a communications network connects these nodes. Again, several options present themselves. We can use dedicated, point-point links. This scheme is limited in scalability by the number of links available, and the interfacing hardware. For example, the Transputer chip comes with 4 dedicated I/O links, each capable of 20 mbps per second each. At the node end, the links terminate in a dma engine that interfaces with the processor's memory. In the case of the Transputer, all of this is on one chip. Similarly, a proprietary chip was used by MPP maker nCube with 16 links for interprocessor communication. The iWarp chip had 4 channels, and the TMS series of RISC-DSP chips had 6. Most of these links are asynchronous serial, but the TI chip had parallel links, limiting the distance between processors. On the other hand, the parallel scheme is faster, and particularly if you plan to pull it all onto one chip as multicore. The MicroBlaze Soft Core processor in a Xininx FPGA can also use the chip's parallel communication resources.

Distributed memory systems come with a "built-in" physical communication scheme between processors. On top of this, we need a communications and messaging protocol, interfaced with the operating system. One approach is the public domain software package PVM (Parallel Virtual Machine).

Speaking of operating systems, we can choose to implement the entire operating system at each node of the distributed memory system, but this uses up a lot of memory. Another approach is to have a kernel at each node, requiring several hundred kbytes, as opposed to 10's of Megabytes. Support for parallel distributed systems is emerging in several operating systems.

In the distributed memory model, there is no requirement to have homogeneous systems. The distributed system resembles a network or a cluster of minicomputers more than one big homogeneous machine. Software such as PVM can link diverse systems across the communications network into one large worker. The next approach would be to have a very fast bus connecting processors with large caches. In fact, we could consider the memory as totally consisting of cache.

The Non-uniform memory access (NUMA) approach is a design for memory architecture in multiprocessing. Local memory is accessed faster that global memory, that referring to another processor's memory, or shared memory. NUMA provides advantages in certain application domains, where data sets are associated with specific tasks. The NUMA approach can be found in certain Operating Systems, such as Unix.

Since processors now operate faster than their memory, they are often starved for data, even with advanced cache architectures. The NUMA approach allocates memory to each processor for its exclusive use, while providing shared memory, and also the ability for a process to access another's memory. The NUMA approach provides cache coherency across processors, by linking the various cache controllers with a communication mechanism NUMA is a type of tightly coupled cluster computing, with virtual memory. NUMA can be instantiated in hardware, or in the Operating System software.

Cache

This section discusses the concept of a cache in generic computer architecture terms. A cache is a temporary memory buffer for data. It is placed between the processor and the main memory. The cache is smaller, but faster than the main memory. Being faster, it is more expensive, so it serves as a transition to the main store. They may be several levels of cache (L1, L2, L3), the one closest to the processor having the highest speed, commensurate to the processor. That closest to the main memory has a lower speed, but is still faster than the main memory. The cache has faster access times, and becomes valuable when items are accessed multiple times. Cache is transparent to the user; it has no specific address.

There can be different caches for instructions and data, or a unified cache for both. Code is usually accessed in linear fashion, but data items are not. In a running program, the code cache is never written, simplifying its design. The nature of accessing for instructions and data is different. On a read access, if the desired item is present in a cache, we get a cache hit, and the item is read. If the item is not in cache, we get a cache miss, and the item must be fetched from memory. There is a small additional time penalty in this process over going directly to memory (in the case of a miss). Cache works because, on the average, we will have the desired item in cache most of the time, by design.

Cache reduces the average access time for data, but will increase the worst-case time. The size and organization of the cache defines the performance for a given program. The proper size and organization is the subject of much analysis and simulation.

Caches introduce indeterminacy in execution time. With cache, memory access time is no longer deterministic. We can't tell, a priori, if an item is or is not in cache. This can be a problem in some real-time systems.

A working set is a set of memory locations used by a program in a certain time interval. This can refer to code or data. Ideally, the working set is in cache. The cache stores not only the data item, but a tag, which identifies where the item is from in main memory. Advanced systems can mark ranges of items in memory as non-cacheable, meaning they are only used once, and don't need to take up valuable cache space.

For best performance, we want to keep frequently-accessed locations in fast cache. Also, cache retrieves more than one word at a time, it retrieves a "line" of data, which can vary in size. Sequential accesses are faster after an initial access (both in cache and regular memory) because of the overhead of set-up times.

Writing data back to cache does not necessarily get it to main memory right away. With a write-through cache, we do immediately copy the written item to main memory. With a write-back cache, we write to main memory only when a location is removed from the cache.

Many locations can map onto the same cache block. Conflict misses are easy to generate: If array A uses locations 0, 1, 2, ... and array b uses locations 1024, 1025, 1026, ..., the operation a[i] + b[i] generates conflict misses in a cache of size 1024.

Caches, then, provide a level of performance increase at the cost of complexity due to temporal or spatial locality of the data. The program is not aware of the location of the data, whether it is in cache or main memory. The only indication is the run time of the program.

Cache hierarchy

This includes the L1, L2, and L3 caches. L1 is the smallest cache, located closest to the CPU, usually on the same chip. Some CPU have all three levels on chip. Each of the levels of cache is a different size and organization, and has different policies, to optimize performance at that point.

A key parameter of cache is the replacement policy. The replacement policy strategy is for choosing which cache entry to overwrite to make room for a new data. There are two popular strategies: random, and least-recently used (LRU). In random, we simply choose a location, write the data back to main memory, and refill the cache from the new desired location. In least recently used scenario, the hardware keeps track of cache accesses, and chooses the least recently used item to swap out.

As long as the hardware keeps track of access, it can keep track of writes to the cache line. If the line has not been written into, it is the same as the items in memory, and a write-back operation is not required. The flag that keeps track of whether the cache line has been written into is called the "dirty" bit. This book does discuss the dirty bits of computer architecture.

Note that we are talking about cache as implemented in random access memory of varying speeds. The concept is the same for memory swapped back and forth to rotating disk; what was called virtual memory in mainframes.

Cache organization

In a fully-associative cache, any memory location can be stored anywhere in the cache. This form is almost never implemented. In a direct-mapped cache, each memory location maps onto exactly one cache entry. In an N-way set-associative cache, each memory location can go into one of n sets. Direct mapped cache has the best hit times. Fully associative cache has the lowest miss rates.

TLB

The Translation Lookaside Buffer (TLB) is a cache used to expedite the translation of virtual to physical memory address. It holds pairs of virtual and translated (physical addresses). If the required translation is present (meaning it was done recently), the process is speeded up.

Caches have a direct effect on performance and determinacy, but the system designer does not always have a choice, when the caches are incorporated as part of the CPU. In this case, the system designer needs to review the cache design choices to ensure it is commensurate with the problem being address by the system.

In a multicore architecture, each core typically includes a certain amount of Level 1 cache, and there is a shared L2 cache. The L2 cache controller access main memory when required. The L1 caches are kept consistent by snooping. This tiered memory approach, with a cpu and up to three levels of cache between it and main memory is the norm. As we get closer to the cpu, the caches get faster, but, necessarily smaller. Caching involves overhead, but the advantage can be significant for preventing data and instruction starvation to a fast cpu core.

Network

Up to about eight processors, a shared bus architecture can work well. Newer schemes use NUMA, non-uniform memory access, which allocates different sections of memory to different processors. Processor accesses to local memory are fast, and to another processor's memory more costly in time.

A Software bus is a model of a shared communication channel among processors, where the hardware part is abstracted.

Clustering

Clustering of computers was an approach people developed to grow their computer resources to fit large problems. If one large mainframe didn't do it, get two. Parallel processing was defined by Gene Amdahl's work at IBM around 1967. Ad hoc clusters required fast data interconnect between the machines A research machine built at Carnegie Mellon University using DEC PDP-11 mini-computers used TCP/IP. The breakthrough was when tools were developed to enable job distribution and file sharing across the cluster. DEC announced their VaxCluster architecture in 1984. This architecture survived the demise of DEC and the Vax architecture, and exists as OpenVMS running on HP's Intel architecture systems. The compute nodes in a cluster can be running non-homogeneous operating systems, as long as everyone can talk the same protocol.

So, we could even do away with some of the weight, and use commodity pc motherboards connected in a cluster architecture. Let's take this a step farther. If we had a pc-on-a-chip, we could make this even smaller, say, a 12" x 12" board with 100 cpu's. Then, with multicore techniques, we can make a cluster on a chip.

Beowulf and PVM

Beowulf is a clustering technique developed at NASA's Goddard Space Flight Center based on commodity pc's as hardware, and the Parallel Virtual Machine (PVM) software, with the linux operating system. These heterogeneous inexpensive clusters provided a virtual supercomputer architecture. This technique came to be known as Grid computing. The Beowulf cluster meant that anyone could build a supercomputer.

The Parallel Virtual Machine (PVM) software package, developed at the Oak Ridge National Laboratory of the Department of Energy, links heterogeneous computers together into one computational resource. It operates on equipment from Sun, Cray, Alliant, IBM, TMC, Intel, and others. The PVM software is Open Source. Customized commercial versions of PVM are available from various vendors.

PVM is transparent to the type of individual machine (shared vs. distributed memory, vector, risc, etc.), and to the interconnect method. PVM software is on each node of the configuration, and presents a virtual, unified computational resource to the user. Library routines for programs in C or Fortran are part of PVM. These routines, when linked with the user code, provide PVM connectivity to the user. Routines are provided for communication and process synchronization.

PVM allows the collection of a number of existing computational resources into one large resource as needed. For example, a heavy use computational job can take advantage of slack or idle time on machines on a network. Alternately, collections of workstations can be linked at night or over the weekend into one large machine to address batch jobs. A graphical interface tool for visualization within the PVM environment is available as HeNCE (Heterogeneous Network Computing Environment).

PVM enabled the linking of inexpensive computation resources such as commodity pc's into supercomputing clusters.

I have a friend who had licensed a piece of NASA software for planetary image enhancement that he wanted to apply in the Medical Imaging field. He couldn't afford a machine to run it, so I suggested a Beowulf Cluster. He built one in his garage, using wooden racks to hold a hundred surplus pc's, coupled by Ethernet, and running the Beowulf cluster software. Not only did it get the job done, he was able to heat his house in Connecticut with the waste heat. Beowulf clusters changed the game in big computing for the masses.

Massively Parallel Systems

Massively parallel systems have hundreds or thousands of cpu's, cooperating on the same problem. The cpu's could be pc's, they could be chips, and now they can be multicore chips.

There are limits to the improvement of program performance in adding more processors. Certainly, we can't have hundreds of people working on this book, with a goal of finishing it in a day. There's too much coordination required. It has been observed that the serial portion of the program, the part that can't be parallelized, doesn't scale. This is referred to as Amdahl's Law. It's like the law of diminishing returns.

Two early chips, both single cpu's, were designed to be the building blocks of massively parallel systems. These were the Inmos Transputer, and the Intel iWarp. Many other early MPS's were build from commodity cpu's, We'll take a look at these to see what made them the ideal component to build a MPS from.

Transputer

The Transputer was a fast single-chip microcomputer requiring a minimum of external support chips. This low cost unit performed on-chip 64-bit floating point processing and had built-in support for parallelism. The key to the understanding of the architecture is the language Occam.

The Transputer itself was a small (1 sq. inch) 84-pin chip, which had a high degree of functional integration. External support requirements were minimal. The Transputer even had 4k bytes of fast RAM on-chip so that minimal systems could be built with no external memory. . The Transputer supported very fast on-chip floating point and had four bi-directional serial links built into the chip, operating at a DMA rate of 20 Mbps each. These links allowed the Transputer to be connected as building blocks into arrays of arbitrary size and complexity. The advantage of the Transputer architecture lay not only in its computation speed, but also in its I/O capacity. A reasonable balance of processing:I/O could be configured for a wide range of applications.

A Transputer had a number of simple operating system functions built into the hardware. These included hardware multitasking with foreground and background priority levels, hardware timers, and hardware time-slicing of background tasks. I/O set-up was extremely simple with this device requiring typically three instructions to initiate DMA read or write across a link with automatic task disabling until I/O completion or timer expiration. Interrupt context switching was also very fast, typically less than one microsecond. In addition, generated code was extremely compact, the most commonly used instructions being only 1 byte long. An OPERATE instruction was included to extend the instruction set. Some models implemented a 2-dimensional block move, clip, and draw. Instructions to calculate CRC on a word, count bits, or reverse bits were also included. Scheduling opcodes were included for starting, running, and stopping a process, as well as priority operations.

A Transputer had I/O resources of four links of 20 megabits/second input and output simultaneously. The links could be hard-wired, jumpered, or connected via the

Inmos C002 32x32 programmable crossbar switch. Each link supported two logical channels in Occam.

The Transputer links provided high speed serial communication between processors and processors and the outside world. Physically, there were three lines per link, input, output, and an associated ground. Each link provided two bi-directional channels, because each wire carried the data for one channel, and the acknowledge for the other. A message was transferred as a sequence as bytes. This meant that word lengths of the sender and receiver did not need to be the same. Acknowledgment was on a per-byte basis.

The four independent serial links on each Transputer supported bi-directional asynchronous communication at TTL levels, and operated concurrently with the integer and floating point engines. Internal to the Transputer chip, the links begin and ended at the OMA engines that operate concurrently with calculations. Thus, it was possible for a Transputer to be executing an integer and a floating point operation, and sending/receiving on 4 channels simultaneously.

The links implemented a point-point protocol, with a separate 32x32 crossbar switch chip (C004) available. Virtual channel architecture could be implemented on the T-800 series, with hardware support in the T-9000 series. T-800 Links support 20 mbps bi-directional communication on a 3 wire medium. Messages were transferred as a series of bytes, with a byte acknowledge. There was a 3-bit per byte overhead on transmission, and the acknowledge packet was two bits in length. The link adapter allowed the interface of 8-bit bi-directional data to the Transputer link protocol, and thus served as a custom uart. It was applicable where interfacing to other communication standards such as MIL-STD-1553 was desired. The crossbar switch allowed the connection among Transputers to be configurable instead of hardwired.

The architecture of the Transputer was ahead of its time, and the complexity of the implementation, and the "alien-ness" of the Occam language prevented widespread use. Occam will be discussed in the software section.

The Transputer remains a good model of an architecture that has a balance of computation and communication.

iWarp

The iWarp was a chip version of Kung's work on a parallel architecture called Warp. The chips were used to build several machines at Carnegie Mellon University, based on the earlier CMMP and CM* projects. Resembling the Transputer, the iWarp was a processor and memory unit that was hooked into networks of communication channels. The original architecture for systolic computing arrays grew out of DARPA's interest in and support via the Strategic Computing Program. The Warp architecture exhibited fine grain parallelism, in the sense of few calculations per I/O.

The goal of the iWarp program was to develop a compute/communicate architecture that would scale in both dimensions. Message passing would exploit worm-hole routing for low overhead. Multiple logical connections on one physical channel would be possible, similar to Inmos' virtual link concept. Fine grained, systolic communication was supported. The iWarp was RISC-like in having a one instruction per clock, with a very long instruction (VLIW) architecture. The iWarp designers strove to achieve a balance between communication and computation, which would address problems spanning the range from fine-grained to coarse grained. In addition, they wanted state-of-the-art vector and scalar performance. Zero overhead communication, like the Transputer's links, was also a goal.

The architecture was systolic, data was pumped in "waves" throughout the processor system, much in the same way that the heart's systolic rhythm pumps blood throughout the body.

The iWarp achieved a communication to computation ratio of 1:1. Each iWarp component consisted of an integer and a floating point computation section, and a communication element. The communication element supported 4 full-duplex I/O channels, of 160 Mbytes/second input and output capability. The computation element supported 20 mips of integer operations, and 20 mFlops of single precision floating point performance. The memory access bandwidth of the computation element was 160 mbytes/second, but there was no memory management (virtual addresses).

The integer execution unit had an 8k rom for initialization and self test. The floating point unit included an adder and multiplier that could operate in parallel. DMA support and interrupts were provided. A timer was included in the architecture.

A communications element integral to the processor was implemented with 8 dma channels. The communication element handled interprocessor data messages. In the message format, 20 bits contained a destination address, 4 bits for message control.

The external memory interface was of a Von Neumann style, with a 64-bit wide data path, and 24-bit address. Since iWarps were designed to be used in large parallel networks, the small address space only effected the size of local memory, not total system memory. A 40 MHz clock was used.

General purpose instructions on the iWarp were 32-bits in size. Following the VLIW philosophy, the iWarp also used a 96-bit compute and access instruction format, with a 32-bit general purpose format. A single VLIW instruction could perform a floating add, floating multiply, two memory address computations, and a memory access. Loop decrement and branch evaluation took two cycles.

The register file contained 128 32-bit locations, It was 15-way ported, and could support 9 reads and 6 writes in one clock time. This feature allowed both the computation agent and communication elements to access the registers simultaneously. The program store unit had a 1 -kilobyte instruction cache, and start-up and system routines in ROM. The integer and floating point units operated in parallel. The floating adder operated in parallel with the multiplier. Single precision required 2 clock cycles, and double precision required 4 cycles from either unit.

Supported data types on the iWarp included bytes, half words, words (32 bit), and double words. iWarp tools were hosted on the Sun platform, and included a C and a Fortran optimizing compiler, with language extensions for parallelism. Support tools also included a linker, debug monitor, and run time environment. Math and Unix system call libraries were available.

Again, a very advanced architecture that didn't get mush traction outside of academia, but contained many good ideas and features to the issue of getting multiple machines to work together.

Symmetric Processing

Symmetric multiprocessing (SMP) involves multiple integral processor units with a common memory, and sharing an operating system. Processors are interconnected with busses, a mesh, point-point, or other communications methods. The bottleneck to scalability is the bandwidth of the interconnect. Mesh schemes avoid this bottleneck, at the cost of complexity, and can provide near linear scalability. The trick is in the programming. Different programming philosophies are required in the multiprocessing environment. If the problem is "embarrassingly parallel," it will scale in terms of the number of resources applied. Pathological non-parallel problems do not scale across multiple resources. Support for SMP is required at the operating systems level, and visibility of the parallelism is necessary at the language level. There is a required paradigm shift on the part of programmers, from the sequential, one thing at a time world, to the parallel, simultaneous approach.

The symmetric part of the architecture allows any processor to be assigned any task. The alternative is to have groups of different architectures, each optimized to a different data structure or task set. In SMP, tasks can be moved around at run time for load balancing.

Asymmetric Processing

In asymmetric multiprocessing, not all cpu's are necessarily treated equally. It was not a particularly useful approach, but served until the technology of SMP was developed. In early mainframe computers, a second cpu could be added, with the primary cpu running the opsys and some user code, and the secondary cpu running only user code. The first cpu supervised the second; the second was acting as a slave processor. The DEC VAX-11/782 is an example, as is the IBM S/370-168.

Multicore Implementations

Multicore processors date from around the year 2000. Coupling between cores is either tight, with shared cache, or loose, with message passing approaches. The on-chip interconnect can be a bus, ring topology, a mesh, torus, or crossbar switch. Homogeneous multi-core consists of the same cores, as in a multi-cpu, multi-dsp, or multi-gpu arrangement. Non-homogeneous uses different cores, such as a mix of cpu's, dsp's, and gpu's.

x86 architectures

Both Intel and AMD have multicore product implementations of the x86 architecture, generally up to 10 cores at this writing, but expanding all the time. The number of cores per chip is expected to follow Moore's Law.

Almost all of the implementations use 2 levels of cache on chip, with each processing element having a private L1 cache, and a shared L2 cache. Each cache controller can do cache snooping (looking in the other caches for changed items) to keep the L1 caches consistent. The L2 cache controller can keep that cache consistent with main memory.

In the Intel implementation of the x86, there is a technique called Hyper-threading, their proprietary simultaneous multi-threading (SMT) parallelization technique. This is effectively virtual multiple cores. Each Intel physical core can be viewed as two virtual cores. This requires support from the operating system. Certain hardware resources are duplicated and others are shared. Multiple hyper-threaded cores can be implemented. The technique is transparent to the operating system, although the operating systems must support SMP to take advantage of the feature. AMD employs a similar technique.

In terms of the mainstream Intel processors, the low-end Atom is dual core, 4-threaded. The mainstream i3, i5, and i7 cpu's are as well, with the i7's being six-core. The Xeon, intended for servers, has 10 cores in the E7 model. The Phi co-processor (discussed below) targets 64 cores.

Intel produced an experimental multicore microprocessor in 2009. This was called the single-chip cloud computer (SCC). It contained 48 of the Pentium P54c cores. The

P54c has dual pipelines, but they are not identical. One does not include the barrel shifter unit. Essentially, each Pentium is a pair of i386's. Without instruction dependencies, the Pentium should be twice as fast as a '386. Because of dependencies, the theoretical number is 1.7 times as fast. In actuality, it is more like 1.2. This is because not every pair of instructions is independent. At the compiler level, the instructions can be re-ordered to improve this, while maintaining logical consistency.

The SCC included a 4x6 2-D mesh architecture for core interconnect. The mesh also connected to four memory controllers, for external DRAM access. Pairs of cores shared a message-passing buffer.

The Intel Multiprocessing approach is called MIC, or Many Integrated Core. This was based on prior work with the SCC, and the Teraflops Research Chip, which was a circa-2007 80-core design. The results of this work to-date is instantiated in the Xeon Phi. This architecture is now in its second generation. The Phi is a co-processor, on a board plugged into a main computer's PCI-X bus. The main cpu runs the main operating system. The Phi has its own version of Linux pre-installed. The Phi board functions as a remote server, as far as your system is concerned, but it is not very remote.

The Intel Xeon Phi co-processor leverages the legacy 32-bit Pentium P54c architecture, replicated in a multicore arrangement, and connected with a ring network. At the moment, they can implement 57 or 61 cores, each with their own L1 caches, and a shared L2 cache. Each core can support 4 hyper-threads. The cores themselves have the dual-issue integer pipelines, and also include the floating point unit. One core is dedicated to running the Linux micro-operating system within the chip. The L1 caches are 32 kbytes, and 8-way set associative. The L2 cache is 512k. A core can execute 16 single precision floating point operation, using an extension to the ISA that allows 512 bit operands. There are 32 of the 512 bit vector registers.

Since the P54c pipelines are not identical, the compiler enforces instruction pairing rules. This is also done in hardware by the instruction dispatcher. Theoretical performance, as calculated by Intel, assumes 60 usable cores operating at 1.1 GHz clock, and delivering more than 2 Teraflops, single precision.

ARM

ARM is an Instruction Set Architecture (ISA) specification. It is instantiated in silicon by numerous companies under license. ARM Holdings PLC, a British Multinational company, is the inheritor of the intellectual property (IP) of the t CPU design, and licenses its use worldwide. The products include the licensable intellectual property for the ARM7, ARM9, ARM11, and the Cortex series. Derivative products include the StrongARM, the Freescale series, the Xscale, the Snapdragon, Samsung's

Hummingbird, the A4 and A5 by Apple, and Texas Instruments products incorporating digital signal processing functionality, among others. This is similar to the situation with Intel's ISA-32, with chips of that architecture built by Intel, and chips with a different implementation of the architecture built by AMD and others. The Intel ISA-16 and ISA-32 addressed the desktop and server market, but embedded versions were also available.

The ARM architecture has at this point more than 700 licenses, and it grows by 100 per year With enough money to cover the licensing fees, anyone can license the ARM design. You can do with it fairly much what you want. The ARM makes a good embedded controller, and is currently found in most mobile phones and tablets. Over 6 billion chips were made in 2010. The latest architecture is targeted to large data center applications. ARM runs GNU/linux-based Android operating system, and the has ports of OpenSolaris, FreeBSD, OpenBSD, NetBSD, and various GNU/linux variations, including Gentoo, Debian, Slackware, and Ubuntu, among others.

The ARM Cortex processors are the latest in the 32-bit series, and extend into multicore and 64-bit models for higher performance. The latest ARM architecture supports multi-core (currently, up to 8-core) architectures. Both symmetrical and asymmetrical implementations are included. Putting a lot of cores on a single substrate is challenging, but getting them to work together co-operatively and non-intrusively is difficult. The CoreLink cache coherent interconnect system IP, for use in multicore applications, is one emerging solution.

Version 8 of the ARM architecture implements 64-bit data structures and addressing, and multi-core. The basic core is dual-issue superscalar (2 execution pipelines), and supports SIMD operation and vector floating point calculations. The architecture can be either symmetrical or asymmetrical. Each core has its own L1 cache, with a shared L2 cache sharing the chip. These chips target the mass server market, in competition with the x86 architecture.

The ARM NEON implements an advanced SIMD instruction set . This is an extension of the FPU with a quad Multiply-and-Accumulate (MAC) unit and additional 64-bit and 128-bit registers.

The Samsung Hummingbird is a system-on-a-chip based on the Cortex A8, and including a GPU. These parts are used in Samsung's Galaxy line of tablets. The Qualcomm Snapdragon chip is based on the Cortex-A8 with the ARM7 instruction set, and includes a GPU. The chip is used in smartphones, tablets, and smart-books. The Snapdragon is produced in dual and quad-core models.

The Cortex-A9 can also have multiple cores that are multi-issue super-scalar and support out-of-order and speculative execution using register renaming. It has an 8-stage pipeline. Two instructions per cycle can be decoded. There are up to 64k of 4-way set associative Level-1 cache, with up to 512k of Level 2. A 64-bit Harvard architecture memory access allows for maximum bandwidth. Four double-word writes take five machine cycles. Floating point units and a media processing engine are available for each core.

The Cortex-A9 micro-architecture comes with either a scalable multi-core processor, the Cortex-A9 MPCore™ multicore processor, or as a more traditional processor, the Cortex-A9 single core processor. The configuration includes 16, 32 or 64KB four-way associative L1 caches, with up to 8MB of L2 cache through the optional L2 cache controller. The memory architecture of the A9 is Harvard, with separate code and data paths. It can sustain four double-word write transfers every 5 cycles. It includes a high efficiency super-scalar pipeline, which removes dependencies between adjacent instructions. It has double the floating point performance of previous units. Up to a 2 GHz clock is currently feasible. Two instructions per cycle are decoded. Instruction execution is speculative, using dynamic register renaming. A similar technique is used to unroll loops in the hardware at execution time. There are four execution pipelines fed from the issue queue, and out-of-order dispatch is supported, as is out-of-order write-back. Items can be marked as non-cachable, or write back or write through.

The Cortex-A9 is implemented in a series of system-on-a-chip devices from multiple manufacturers. As an example, the STMElectronics SPEAr1310 is a dual-core Cortex-A SMP. It has dual cores, and can support either symmetric or asymmetric multiprocessing. It has a 32k instruction and a 32k data cache at Level 1. The Level 2 cache is unified, and is 512k bytes in size. The on-chip interprocessor bus is 64 bits wide.

The Cortex-A15 is multi-core, and has an out-of-order super-scalar pipeline. The chip was introduced in 2012, and is available from TI, NVidia, Samsung, and others. It can address a terabyte of memory. The integer pipeline is 15 stages long, and the floating point pipeline is up to 25 stages. The instruction issue is speculative. There can be 4 cores per cluster, two clusters per chip. Each core has separate 32k data and instruction caches. The level-2 cache controller supports up to 4 megabytes per cluster. DSP and NEON SIMD are supported, as is floating point. Hardware virtualization support is included.

CUDA

CUDA (Compute Unified Device Architecture) is a trademark of nVidia Corporation. It is a parallel computing platform and a programming model. It enables dramatic increases in computing performance by harnessing the power of the graphics processing unit (GPU). A CUDA program includes parallel functions (kernels) across parallel threads. The compiler organizes these threads into blocks and grids. A block is a set of concurrently executing threads that can synchronize and co-ordinate. A grid is an array of blocks. The CUDA programming model a thread has private memory. Each block has shared memory space, as do Grids.

Threads map to processors. Each Gpu unit executes one or more grids. Each streaming multiprocessor executes one or more thread blocks, and CUDA cores, and possibly other execution engines execute threads.

CUDA introduced a variation on the digital signal processing Multiply-Accumulate operation (AxB+C), called Fused Multiply-ADD (FMA). In traditional Multiply-Add the AxB product will be truncated, but in the FMA, all bits of the produce are retained for the ADD operation.

Applying the horsepower of the GPU to real problems, the CUDA allows applications to be written in c, c++, Python and FORTRAN. NVIDIA unveiled CUDA in 2006 as a solution for general-computing on GPU's.

The G-80 chip, introduced in 2006, established the GPU computing model. It supported the c programming language, and was threaded. It implemented the Single Instruction, Multiple thread concept. It had a complexity of 680 million-1.4 billion transistors. It did not include L1 or L2 cache.

Fermi

The Fermi architecture was released in 2010, as a significant improvement over the G-80. It implemented up to 512 CUDA cores, each executing an integer or floating point operation pr clock. CUDA cores, and required 3 billion transistors. The chip supported c++, OpenCL, and DirectCompute. It featured full IEEE floating point, single and double precision. It implemented on chip L1 and L2 caches. The GigaThread^{tm} engine allowed for concurrent kernel execution, and out-of-order thread block execution. Both L1 and L2 cache were included. The architecture was 32-bit. A new instruction set architecture (ISA) supported parallel thread execution via a virtual machine.

Kepler

The Kepler GK110 CUDA chip is constructed from over 7 billion transistors, and provides a TeraFlop (10^{12}) of double-precision floating point operations per second. This is a performance increase of a factor of three over its predecessor, the Fermi model. The high-end model includes dynamic parallelism, which adjusts and controls the scheduling in the GU without the intervention of the CPU. GPU utilization is enhanced by a technique known as Hyper-Q, which allows multiple cpu cores to use a single GPU, up to 32.

The unit can include up to 15 SMX processor units, and six 64-bit memory controllers. There is a 1536 kbytes of L2 Cache on chip. SMX is nVidia's term for the Streaming Microprocessor architecture. SMX has 8 instruction dispatch engines, a 32-bit register files of size 65,536, 64 kbytes of shared memory/L1 cache, and a 48k read-only data cache. This cache is reserved for data values known (by the compiler) not to change, and thus no cache writes are required. It also includes 192 CUDA cores, 64 double-precision arithmetic units, 32 special function units (SFU), and 32 load/store units. The CUDA cores include both integer and floating point capability,. The special function units assist in transcendental computations.

A group of 32 threads than can operate in parallel is called a warp. Up to 4 warps can be executing simultaneously. Thread scheduling is done in hardware, but based on information from the compiler ("hints') concerning dependencies and data hazards. The compiler is a critical part of scheduling threads for best efficiency. The threads are allocated up to 255 per thread. A special instruction allows executing threads to share data without going through shared memory. Atomic memory operations are provided to ensure consistency among threads.

Texture filtering units (TFU's) are provided in the architecture, with each SMS having 16.

All on-chip memory is single-error-correct, double-error-detect. If a cache line is found to be invalid, a new read operation is automatically generated. Fetches from external DRAM are protected by an error-correcting code.

MicroBlaze Cluster on a Chip

Would you rather build your own multi-core chips? Well, you can do that, with a FPGA, and soft-core cpu's. The soft-core is a data file, containing configuration information for putting the cpu into the memory and logic fabric of the FPGA. You can even configure some of its parameters. In addition, more than one will fit, so you can have a multiprocessor.

In a Xilinx FPGA, the softcore processor of choice is the Microblaze, a 32-bit architecture with an associated floating point unit and eight of Xilinx's high speed 32-bit links, know as FSL (Fast Simplex link). Compare this to the Transputer architecture, which had 4 full duplex serial links. The Xilinx links are point-to-point. Using parallel instead of serial means that a switching scheme is cumbersome. However, the links achieve a transfer rate of 300 Mbytes/second. With 8 links, the topology of the Multiprocessor is limited. A completely meshed network, each processor connected to each other, would only work for 9 Microblaze processor nodes,. A ring network is possible, and provides unlimited connectivity, but has issues with distance between the transmitter and receiver, and each compute node must also be a re-transmitter. We could also implement a star network, where there is a central processor, through which all communication goes. So, it doesn't get much chance to participate in computation. A star network would be limited to 8 devices. A linked star network would also be possible, with the central nodes linked.

For eight Microblaze architectures, only a 15% usage of available logic building blocks was used in an early Virtex-2 architecture. The bottleneck in this implementation was the amount of ram available on-chip for the processors.

Now, with more ram available in the newest generation of chips, each processor can run a port of Linux.

Others

Texas Instruments offers a range of multicore products, based on several of their chip families. The Open Multimedia Applications Platform (OMAP) family are processors for audio and video data. These are non-homogeneous multicore chips, with a general purpose ARM cpu, and one or more specialized co-processors. OMAP-5 is the latest generation. These use the ARM Cortex-A15 with two additional ARM Cortex-M4 cores, 2 graphics cores, a graphics engine, and a signal processor. These address high definition video displays and processing, including 3-D. Less complex OMAP processors are found in mobile phones and tablets.

TI's TMS320 series are DSP chips. There are versions with one to six DSP cores. The cores are the TMS320c54x models, or theTMS320C64x, which features VLIW technology.

Picochip was acquired by Mindspeed Technologies, along with its product lines, including multicore digital signal processing units. The picoArray has up to 300 dsp cores on a single die. Each is a 16-bit Harvard architecture processor implementing VLIW, and local memory. The interconnect mechanism uses message passing with a mesh arrangement. The specific interconnects are fixed at compile time, and are not dynamically changeable. This implements the Communicating Sequential Process model, like the Transputer. Each process maps to an independent processor. The company maintains the IP as a licensable product, and uses the design itself for a wireless infrastructure product, the femto-cell. This is a small cell site.

Freescale is a licensee of the ARM processor Intellectual Property, and a major manufacturer of variations of the ARM, including multi-core. They also have the QorlQ B3421 processor, which includes two dual-thread 64-bit POWER architecture CPU's and two vector processor cores. The POWER architecture is RISC, controlled by the organization Power.org, and built by Freescale, IBM, and others. The chip is intended for radio applications, such as cell stations. The POWER cores include a AltiVec 128-bit SIMD engine, and 1 megabyte of cache for sharing between cores. The vector processors can execute up to 8 instructions per clock cycle, on vector data. They have 2 megabytes of cache, for sharing between cores. The shared caches for the dual processor types (POWER and VPU) lead to an on-chip 512k L3 cache. All cores have a 32k D-cache, and a 32-k I-cache.

Multicore Embedded

Multicore techniques are now being applied to embedded processors as well. This enables some techniques that were not previously available. In the embedded world, the cores do not necessarily need to be the same. Actually, this technique was used when to Intel floating point co-processor, the 80387, was incorporated onto the same chip as the integer processor, the 80386, in the design of the follow-on 80486 chip. Today, multiple integer cores can share the same silicon substrate with specialized floating point, digital signal and vector processing, and specialized media and video engines. The individual cores can implement superscalar, super-pipelined, or other optimization techniques. Essentially, we will shortly have a MIMD (multiple instruction, multiple data) parallel processing chip for embedded applications. Nothing is ever free, though. The challenge, as always, will be the programming.

Parallel and Concurrent Programming Languages

The main problem remains in coming up with a way to explicitly express the inherent parallelism of the problem in a computer language. Standard computer languages are serial control flow or data flow, or a mix, but are not good at expressing parallelism. Extensions to standard languages such as c also exist as parallel c.

A concurrent language handles simultaneously executing processes or threads. A Parallel language can handle programs that simultaneously execute on more than one processor (or core).

Examples of fine-grained task-parallel languages can be found more in the area of Hardware Description Languages like Verilog and VHDL, which represent a code-static approach paradigm where the program has a static structure and the data is changing. This is in contrast to a data static model where the data is not changing but the algorithm does change. These languages are used to describe a hardware implementation of a processing entity, for example, in an FPGA. They are sometimes referred to as logic programming languages.

In FPGA design, we would like to compile a standard programming language, such as c, directly to hardware.

Actually, tools exist to do this. The problem remains, the c language, and other "serial" languages, do not correctly express the inherent and intended parallelism in the problem.

The Occam Language

Occam provides the conceptual framework, and the tools for expressing and programming parallelism. Super-scalar machines exploit independent execution of multiple execution units to achieve a low-level parallelism to break the one-instruction-per-clock limit per package. Certain classes of problems decompose easily into autonomous subtasks for simultaneous execution on vector machines. Vectorizing compilers ferret out this latent parallelism from inherently sequential process. The Occam language forces us to program in parallel, a mindset switch that does not come easily, but is worth the effort. Explicit parallelism in the instantiation of the program leads to the best results. Existing languages such as C may be extended with parallel constructs to ease the programmer transition to this new paradigm. Granularity of the process refers to the size or level that we decompose the parent process into. The level of granularity effects the computation to communication ratio.

A ten person-week task is done by 1 person in ten weeks, but can't necessarily be done by 10 persons in 1 week, or by a staff of 400 in one day. Coarse-grained parallelism (an example is the Mandelbrot set calculation) refers to processes that are largely independent, and require little or no communication. Fine grained decomposition results in more and smaller portions in greater level of detail, with a correspondingly higher need for communication. For example, attempting to decompose the Mandelbrot set calculation below the processor per pixel limit would have separate processors for the real and imaginary parts of the equation, with a need for communication bandwidth sufficient to form the absolute value of the complex number for comparison against a limit.

Problems have an intrinsic granularity that maps best to a particular processor topology. Then, the communication and interaction between processes must be determined. Generally, as the granularity is increased, the need for communication is increased. In Occam, a channel is the communication mechanism between processes. Among processes on one Transputer, the number of virtual channels is unlimited. Between Transputer's, the channels were mapped to the four available physical hardware links.

The origin of the name Occam is traced to the 14th century Sir William of Occam, who's principle of Occam's razor literally translated from the Latin says "entities must not be multiplied beyond what is necessary', or, in the vernacular, "kiss: keep it simple, stupid". What William was trying to say was, of two or more solutions or approaches always choose the simplest. In the language Occam, an independent task is a collection of simple or atomic tasks and events. A process is mapped to one or more processors.

Concurrent processes were completely independent, can run simultaneously, and have no shared variables. Processes communicate via channels. Channels map to hardware links, and processes were implemented as software entities in Occam.

Occam is a language that makes the description of the parallelism of the problem easier. It is a structured system description language. It had many features of popular programming languages, but extends these with the PAR constructor, which directs execution of operations in parallel. Occam is the language that implements the concept of Communicating Sequential Processes (CSP). The Occam model of concurrency uses processes that run independently, and communicate with other processes. Occam can also implement simple sequential processes. Parallelism is then like a pipeline of processes.

The Transputer hardware instantiates the Occam concurrency model. This leads to an architecture that is ideal for real-time control applications.

The Occam language implements a simple syntax both for parallel processes, and for communication between processes. Multiple processes could be implemented on one processor or on multiple processors. The communication method at the software level was the same. On one Transputer there was virtual concurrency, and one multiple Transputer's there was real concurrency of processes.

Concurrent processes are executed using a linked list approach. A process could be active or inactive. An active process are executing or awaiting execution. An inactive process, which consumes no processor time, can be waiting for I/O resources, or for a particular time to execute.

Versions of Occam for different architectures still exist. One is the Occam-pi open source process language, which comes with a virtual machine for the Intel architecture. Its CCSP scheduler handles multiple processes across multiple processors. An Occam/CSP extension to Python also exists.

Other parallel languages

There are many other programming languages that address the parallelization of resources such as the cpu. These include languages that explicitly express the parallelism of the problem, as well as extensions to common programming languages with parallelism features built-in.

Java supports a multi-threaded architecture, which can be mapped to multiple execution engines. Parallel-c has extensions to the language to allow aspects of parallelism to be expressed. So does some variations of Fortran and Modula. There is also a Concurrent Pascal. Application languages such as LabView support parallelism. LabView has a dataflow architecture that maps well to parallel hardware.

Parallel-C supports architectures with the SMP/NUMA architecture, as well as the distributed memory model, like clusters. It is built on ISO-C, but includes an explicitly parallel execution model with a shared address space. It provides synchronization primitives and memory consistency. There are features for memory management and communications. Previously, Parallel-C operated with a pre-processor to first examine and exploit the parallelism of the problem. Unified Parallel C comes from the High Performance Computing Laboratory of the George Washington University.

Another language option is Co-array Fortran, an extension of Fortran-95. Fortran is alive and well, a favorite of big computation users. Coarray Fortran operates as if were replicated, and each copy executes simultaneously, with its own set of data.

nVidia's CUDA provides a parallel environment for GPU's. To go along with the hardware, nVidia provided massively parallel CDA-c, OpenCL, and DirectCompute software tools. These support not only parallelization, but also debugging of parallel code. GPU-trageted code can be developed by the same process and with the same look-and-feel tools as CPU code. Nvidia's Nexus development environment supported Microsoft Visual Studio, and C++.

We must consider the software tools to develop parallel applications to be of equal or greater importance than the hardware. We would like to have canned libraries of vector and matrix operations. We also could use vectorizing pre-processing compilers.

Vectorizing Compilers

The vectorizer pre-processes source code to convert standard statements and calls into vector processing calls from a supplied library. These library functions make maximal use of the specific pipeline and parallel architecture of the chip. Generally, a data dependency analysis is performed on loops to identify sections to be converted to library calls. The library must then be linked to the compiled code. The vectorizer must sometimes remove scalar optimization, which can mask vectorization.

Taking advantage of the vector libraries optimizes performance and throughput, and allows achievement of the full pipeline efficiency and multiple execution per clock potential of the hardware.

In multicore, vectorizing takes place at the core level. It allows you to apply SIMD techniques to vector data. For example, we might have a vector (just a data structure, really) of six, 32-bit items. These are all associated, first in the problem, but also in memory as one 48 byte entity. We might want to add two of these vectors, or multiply them. We're just applying the same operations to multiple entries in a ordered set of data – SIMD. Vectorization may be local to the core, but can be implemented in parallel fashion across multiple processors as well.

Task Parallelism

Task parallelism is an approach to spread threads or processes across multiple processors. It is control parallelism, not data-parallelism. If each processor executes a different thread on the same or different data, and the threads can communicate, we have achieved parallelism. Not all programs can run in this manner. The Java Virtual Machine implements task parallelism.

Java is an object-oriented language with a syntax similar to that of c. The language is compiled to byte codes, which are executed by a Java Virtual Machine (JVM). The JVM is hosted on the computer hardware, and is an instruction interpreter program. Thus, the Java language is independent of the hardware it executes on. The JVM has also been instantiated directly in hardware.

The JVM is a software environment that allows bytecodes to be executed. There are standard libraries to implement the applications programming interface (API). These implement the Java runtime environment. Other languages besides Java can be compiled into bytecodes, notably Pascal, ADA, and Python. JVM is written in the c language.

The JVM can emulate and interpret the instruction set, or use a technique called Just in Time (JIT) compilation. The latter approach provides greater speed. The JVM also validates the bytecodes before execution.

 The bytecode is interpreted or compiled. Java includes an API to make up the Java runtime environment. Oracle Corporation owns Java, but allows use of the trademark, as long as the products adhere to the JVM Specification. The JVM implements a stack-based architecture. Code executes as privileged or unprivileged, which limits access to some resources.

Intel supports their Multicore hardware with a variety of tools, including Parallel Studio XE. This includes 4 tools, called Composer, VTune Amplifer, Advisor, and Inspector. Composer supplies the C++ and Fortran compiler, the math libraries, and the thread Building Blocks. The Advisor looks over your code, and suggests areas that could be accelerated by parallelism. The Vtune tool profiles running code, to identify hotspots, where more optimization might be applied. The inspector looks for parallel problems such as threading errors, and memory problems. The maturity of the Studio tool, coupled with the large amount of user experience, makes it fairly easy for a programmer new to parallelism.

Large application packages such as National Instrument's LabView are multicore aware, and support support these features in a graphics development environment.

Software licensing issues

Proprietary software is usually licensed per processor. Do you need multiple licenses for each instance in a multi-core implementation? Microsoft says, they license per socket. Check this issue before proceeding with Operation System or Application Packages. The Adobe policy on multi-core licensing states that every 2 core processors on a multi-core machine are equivalent to one CPU from a licensing perspective. Multicore support in Open Software applications such as OpenOffice is generally available, and not an issue.

Open Source vs. Proprietary

This is a topic we need to discuss before we get too far into software. It is not a technical topic, but concerns your right to use (and/or own, modify) software. It's those software licenses you click to agree with, and never read. That's what the intellectual property lawyers are betting on.

Software and software tools are available in proprietary and open source versions. Open source software is free and widely available, and may be incorporated into your system. It is available under license, which generally says that you can use it, but derivative products must be made available under the same license. This presents a problem if it is mixed with purchased, licensed commercial software, or a level of exclusivity is required. Major government agencies such as the Department of Defense and NASA have policies related to the use of Open Source software.

Adapting a commercial or open source operating system to a particular problem domain can be tricky. Usually, the commercial operating systems need to be used "as-is" and the source code is not available. The software can usually be configured between well-defined limits, but there will be no visibility of the internal workings. For the open source situation, there will be a multitude of source code modules and libraries that can be configured and customized, but the process is complex. The user can also write new modules in this case.

Large corporations or government agencies sometimes have problems incorporating open source products into their projects. Open Source did not fit the model of how they have done business traditionally. They are issues and lingering doubts. NASA has created an open source license, the NASA Open source Agreement (NOSA), to address these issues. It has released software under this license, but the Free Software Foundation has some issues with the terms of the license. The Open Source Initiative (www.opensource.org) maintains the definition of Open Source, and certifies licenses such as the NOSA.

The GNU General Public License (GPL) is the most widely used free software license. It guarantees end users the freedoms to use, study, share, copy, and modify the software. Software that ensures that these rights are retained is called free software. The license was originally written by Richard Stallman of the Free Software Foundation (FSF) for the GNU project in 1989. The GPL is a copyleft license, which means that derived works can only be distributed under the same license terms. This is in distinction to permissive free software licenses, of which the BSD licenses are the standard examples. Copyleft is in counterpoint to traditional copyright. Proprietary software "poisons" the free software, and cannot be included or integrated with it, without abandoned the GPL. The GPL cover the GNU/linux operating systems and most of the GNU/linux-based applications.

A Vendor's software tools and Operating system or application code is usually proprietary intellectual property. It is unusual to get the source code to examine, at least without binding legal documents and additional funds. Along with this, you get the vendor support. An alternative is open source code, which is in the public domain. There are a series of licenses covering open source code usage, including the Creative Commons License, the gnu public license, copyleft (alternative to copyright), and others. Open Source describes a collaborative environment for development and testing. Use of open source code carries with it an implied responsibility to "pay back" to the community. Open Source is not necessarily free.

The Open source philosophy is sometimes at odds with the rigid-ized procedures evolved to ensure software performance and reliability. Offsetting this is the increased visibility into the internals of the software packages, and control over the entire software package. Besides application code, operating systems such as GNU/linux and bsd can be open source. The programming language Python is open source. The popular web server Apache is also open source.

Afterword

Multicore technology is a game-changer, and has provided an opportunity to re-think applications that were previous discarded as impractical. In 2011, NASA's Office of the Chief Technologist, as part of the Game Changing Technology Program, issued a Request for Information (RFI) for new computing architectures for space flight use. The study identified the development of Rad-Hard multi-core Processors for aerospace applications as a key technology. So, shortly, Multicore will not be confined to this planet alone.

With a modern Multicore cpu, and a toolset like Parallel Studio XE, you, at home, have access to tools that were reserved for national-level labs, just a few years ago. To say this will result in an explosion of development in large yet inexpensive parallel computers with massive capabilities to tackle problem domains thought too hard to manage, is an understatement.

Glossary of Terms and Acronyms

1's complement – a binary number representation scheme for negative values.

2's complement – another binary number representation scheme for negative values.

Accumulator – a register to hold numeric values during and after an operation.

ACM – Association for Computing Machinery; professional organization.

Ada – a programming language named after Ada Augusta, Countess of Lovelace, and daughter of Lord Byron; arguably, the first programmer. Collaborator with Charles Babbage.

ALU – arithmetic logic unit.

ANSI – American National Standards Institute

API – application program interface; specification for software modules to communicate.

ARM – 32bit computer architecture.

ArpaNet – Advanced Research Projects Agency (U.S.), first packet switched network, 1968.

ASCII - American Standard Code for Information Interchange, a 7-bit code; developed for teleprinters.

ASIC – application specific integrated circuit, custom or semi-custom,.

Assembly language – low level programming language specific to a particular ISA.

Async – asynchronous; using different clocks.

Babbage, Charles –early 19th century inventor of mechanical computing machinery to solve difference equations, and output typeset results; later machines would be fully programmable.

Barrel shifter – logic unit that can shift a data word any number of places in one clock cycle.

Baud – symbol rate; may or may not be the same as bit rate.

BCD – binary coded decimal. 4-bit entity used to represent 10 different decimal digits; with 6 spare states.

Big-endian – data format with the most significant bit or byte at the lowest address, or transmitted first.

Binary – using base 2 arithmetic for number representation.

BIOS – basic input output system; first software run after boot.

BIST – built-in self test.

Bit – smallest unit of digital information; two states.

Blackbox – functional device with inputs and outputs, but no detail on the internal workings.

Boolean – a data type with two values; an operation on these data types; named after George Boole, mid-19th century inventor of Boolean algebra.

Bootstrap – a startup or reset process that proceeds without external intervention.

Buffer – a temporary holding location for data.

Bug – an error in a program or device.

Bus – data channel, communication pathway for data transfer.

Byte – ordered collection of 8 bits; values from 0-255

C – programming language from Bell Labs, circa 1972.

Cache – faster and smaller intermediate memory between the processor and main memory.

Cache coherency – process to keep the contents of multiple caches consistent,

Cache snooping – a technique to check other caches for changed items.

CAS – column address strobe (in DRAM refreshing)

Chip – integrated circuit component.

Clock – periodic timing signal to control and synchronize operations.

Cluster – a multiprocessor using communication resources between processing units.

CMOS – complementary metal oxide semiconductor; a technology using both positive and negative   to achieve low power operation.

Complement – in binary logic, the opposite state.

Compilation – software process to translate source code to assembly or machine code (or error codes).

Control Flow – computer architecture involving directed flow through the program; data dependent paths are allowed.

Co-processor – another processor to supplement the operations of the main processor. Used for floating point, video, etc. Usually relies on the main processor for instruction fetch; and control.

Core – early non-volatile memory technology based on ferromagnetic toroid's. Also, a modular processor unit, like a cpu.

Cots – commercial, off-the-shelf.

CPU – central processing unit.

CRC – cyclic redundancy code, an error-control mechanism.

Crossbar switch – allowing any unit to talk to any other, like a telephone exchange.

CSP – Communicating Sequential Processes, a model for parallelism.

CUDA - Compute Unified Device Architecture; parallel programming framework by NVIDIA.

DARPA – Defense Advanced Research Projects Agency

Dataflow – computer architecture where a changing value forces recalculation of dependent values.

Datagram – message on a packet switched network; the delivery, arrival time, and order of arrival are not guaranteed.

D-cache – data cache

DDR – dual data rate (memory).

Deadlock – a situation in which two or more competing actions are each waiting for the other to finish, and thus neither ever does.

DCE – data communications equipment; interface to the network.

Denorm – in floating point representation, a non-zero number with a magnitude less than the smallest normal number.

Device driver – specific software to interface a peripheral to the operating system.

Digital – using discrete values for representation of states or numbers.

Dirty bit – used to signal that the contents of a cache have changed.

DMA - direct memory access (to/from memory, for I/O devices).

Double word – two words; if word = 8 bits, double word = 16 bits.

Dram – dynamic random access memory.

DTE – data terminal equipment; communicates with the DCE to get to the network.

DVI – digital visual interface (for video).

ECL – emitter coupled logic, a bipolar transistor logic that is fast and power hungry.

EIA – Electronics Industry Association.

Embedded (computer, processor) – cpu with associated I/O and memory, part of a larger system.

Epitaxial – in semiconductors, have a crystalline over-layer with a well-defined orientation.

Eprom – erasable programmable read-only memory.

EEprom – electrically erasable read-only memory.

Ethernet – 1980's networking technology. IEEE 802.3.

Exception – interrupt due to internal events, such as overflow.

FET – field effect transistor.

Fetch/execute cycle – basic operating cycle of a computer; fetch the instruction, execute the instruction.

Firewire – serial communications protocol (IEEE-1394).

Firmware – code contained in a non-volatile memory.

Fixed point – computer numeric format with a fixed number of digits or bits, and a fixed radix point.

Flag – a binary indicator.

Flash memory – a type of non-volatile memory, similar to EEprom.

Flip-flop – a circuit with two stable states; ideal for binary.

Floating point – computer numeric format for real numbers; has significant digits and an exponent.

FPGA – field programmable gate array.

FPU – floating point unit, an ALU for floating point numbers.

Full duplex – communication in both directions simultaneously.

Gate – a circuit to implement a logic function; can have multiple inputs, but a single output.

Giga - 10^9 or 2^{30}

GPU – graphics processing unit. ALU for graphics data.

GUI – graphics user interface.

Half-duplex – communications in two directions, but not simultaneously.

Handshake – co-ordination mechanism.

Harvard architecture – memory storage scheme with separate instructions and data.

Hexadecimal – base 16 number representation.

Hexadecimal point – radix point that separates integer from fractional values of hexadecimal numbers.

Hyperthreading – an Intel approach to multithreading, involving virtual cores.

I-cache – instruction cache

IDE – Integrated development environment for software.

IEEE – Institute of Electrical and Electronic Engineers. Professional organization and standards body.

IEEE-754 – standard for floating point representation and operations.

Infinity - the largest number that can be represented in the number system.

Integer – the natural numbers, zero, and the negatives of the natural numbers.

Interrupt – an asynchronous event to signal a need for attention (example: the phone rings).

Interrupt vector – entry in a table pointing to an interrupt service routine; indexed by interrupt number.

I/O – Input-output from the computer to external devices, or a user interface.

IP – intellectual property; also internet protocol.

IPC – Inter Processor Connect

ISA – instruction set architecture, the software description of the computer.

ISA-32 – 32 bit instruction set architecture

ISA-64 = 64-bit instruction set architecture

ISO – International Standards Organization.

ISR – interrupt service routine, a subroutine that handles a particular interrupt event.

JTAG – Joint Test Action Group; industry group that lead to IEEE 1149.1, Standard Test Access Port and Boundary-Scan Architecture.

Junction – in semiconductors, the boundary interface of the n-type and p-type material.

Kernel – main portion of the operating system. Interface between the applications and the hardware.

Kilo – a prefix for 10^3 or 2^{10}

LAN – local area network.

L1 – fast, small cache memory closest to the CPU

L2 – larger cache between the L1 cache and the main memory.

Latency – time delay.

List – a data structure.

Little-endian – data format with the least significant bit or byte at the highest address, or transmitted last.

Logic operation – generally, negate, AND, OR, XOR, and their inverses.

Loop-unrolling – optimization of a loop for speed at the cost of space.

LRU – least recently used; an algorithm for item replacement in a cache.

LSB – least significant bit or byte.

LUT – look up table.

Mac – media access control; a mac address is unique on a network.

Machine language – native code for a particular computer hardware.

Mainframe – a computer you can't lift.

Mantissa – significant digits (as opposed to the exponent) of a floating point value.

Master-helper – control process with one element in charge. Master status may be exchanged among elements.

Math operation – generally, add, subtract, multiply, divide.

Mega - 10^6 or 2^{20}

Memory leak – when a program uses memory resources but does not return them, leading to a lack of available memory.

Memory scrubbing – detecting and correcting bit errors.

Mesh – a highly connected network.

MESI – modified, exclusive, shared, invalid state of a cache coherency protocol.

Metaprogramming – programs that produce or modify other programs.

Microcode – hardware level data structures to translate machine instructions into sequences of circuit level operations.

Microcontroller – microprocessor with included memory and/or I/O.

Microkernel – operating system which is not monolithic. Functions execute in user space.

Microprocessor – a monolithic cpu on a chip.

Microprogramming – modifying the microcode.

MIL-STD-1553 – military standard (US) for a serial communications bus for avionics.

MIMD – multiple instruction, multiple data

Minicomputer – smaller than a mainframe, larger than a pc.

Minix – Unix-like operating system; free and open source.

MIPS – millions of instructions per second; sometimes used as a measure of throughput.

MISD – multiple instruction, single data.

MMU – memory management unit; translates virtual to physical addresses.

MPP - Massively Parallel Processor.

MPSoC – Multiprocessor System on a chip

MPU – memory protection unit – like an MMU, but without address translation.

MRAM – Magnetorestrictive random access memory. Non-volatile memory approach using magnetic storage elements and integrated circuit fabrication techniques.

MSB – most significant bit or byte.

Multiplex – combining signals on a communication channel by sampling.

Multiprocessing – using more than one processor.

Mutex – a data structure and methodology for mutual exclusion.

Multi-threading – running multiple threads simultaneously

Multicore – multiple processing cores on one substrate or chip; need not be identical.

Multi-processor – Computer with more than one compute engine.

NAN – not-a-number; invalid bit pattern.

NAND – negated (or inverse) AND function.

NASA – National Aeronautics and Space Administration.

NDA – non-disclosure agreement; legal agreement protecting IP.

Nibble – 4 bits, ½ byte.

NIST – National Institute of Standards and Technology (US), previously, National Bureau of Standards.

NMI – non-maskable interrupt; cannot be ignored by the software.

NOR – negated (or inverse) OR function

Normalized number – in the proper format for floating point representation.

Null modem – acting as two modems, wired back to back. Artifact of the RS-232 standard.

NUMA – non-uniform memory access for multiprocessors; local and global memory access protocol.

Nvidia – high-performance video card company.

NVM – non-volatile memory.

Octal – base 8 number.

Off-the-shelf – commercially available; not custom.

OMAP - Open Multimedia Applications Platform

Opcode – part of a machine language instruction that specifies the operation to be performed.

Open source – methodology for hardware or software development with free distribution and access.

Opsys - Operating system – software that controls the allocation of resources in a computer.

OSI – Open systems interconnect model for networking, from ISO.

Overflow - the result of an arithmetic operation exceeds the capacity of the destination.

Packet – a small container; a block of data on a network.

Paging – memory management technique using fixed size memory blocks.

Paradigm – a pattern or model.

Paradigm shift – a change from one paradigm to another. Can be disruptive or evolutionary.

Parallel – multiple operations or communication proceeding simultaneously.

Parallel language – computer language with constructs to express parallelism.

Parallel Processor – computer capable of multiple simultaneous operations.

Parity – an error detecting mechanism involving an extra check bit in the word.

PC – personal computer, politically correct, program counter.

PCB – printed circuit board.

PCI – peripheral interconnect interface (bus).

PCMCIA - Personal Computer Memory Card International Association, small card for memory expansion.

PDA – personal digital assistant. Small, hand-held computer like the Palm Pilot.

PE – processor element.

Peta - 10^{15} or 2^{50}

Pinout – mapping of signals to I/O pins of a device.

Pipeline – operations in serial, assembly-line fashion.

Pixel – picture element; smallest addressable element on a display or a sensor.

Posix – portable operating system interface, IEEE standard.

PROM – programmable read-only memory.

PVM – Parallel virtual machine, open source software to implement clusters.

Quad word – four words. If word = 16 bits, quad word is 64 bits.

Queue – first in, first out data buffer structure; hardware of software.

RAID – random array of inexpensive disks; using commodity disk drives to build large storage arrays.

Radix point – separates integer and fractional parts of a real number.

RAM – random access memory; any item can be access in the same time as any other.

RAS – Row address strobe, in dram refresh.

Register – temporary storage location for a data item.

Reset – signal and process that returns the hardware to a known, defined state.

RISC – reduced instruction set computer.

ROM – read only memory.

Router – networking component for packets.

Real-time – system that responds to events in a predictable, bounded time.

RS-232 – EIA telecommunications standard (1962), serial with handshake.

SAM – sequential access memory, like a magnetic tape.

SATA – serial ATA, a storage media interconnect.

Sandbox – an isolated and controlled environment to run untested or potentially malicious code.

SCI – Scalable Computer Interconnect, IEEE Std 1596-1992.

SDRAM – synchronous dynamic random access memory.

Segmentation – dividing a network or memory into sections.

Self-modifying code – computer code that modifies itself as it runs; hard to debug

Semiconductor – material with electrical characteristics between conductors and insulators; basis of current technology processor and memory devices.

Semaphore –signaling element among processes.

Serial – bit by bit.

Server – a computer running services on a network.

Shift – move one bit position to the left or right in a word.

Sign-magnitude – number representation with a specific sign bit.

Signed number – representation with a value and a numeric sign.

SIMD – single instruction, multiple data.

SIMT - Single Instruction, Multiple Thread.

Simm – single in-line memory module.

SISD – single instruction, single data.

SMP – symmetric multiprocessing.

SMT - simultaneous multi-threading.

Snoop – monitor packets in a network, or data in a cache.

SOC – system-on-chip.

Soft Core – a cpu core IP instantiated in an FPGA

Software – set of instructions and data to tell a computer what to do.

SRAM – static random access memory.

Stack – first in, last out data structure. Can be hardware of software.

Stack pointer – a reference pointer to the top of the stack.

State machine – model of sequential processes.

Supercomputer – a computer more capable than you have, and more expensive than you can afford.

Superscalar – computer with instruction-level parallelism, by replication of resources.

Synchronous – using the same clock to coordinate operations.

System – a collection of interacting elements and relationships with a specific behavior.

Table – data structure. Can be multi-dimensional.

Tera - 10^{12} or 2^{40}

Test-and-set – coordination mechanism for multiple processes that allows reading to a location and writing it in a non-interruptable manner.

TCP/IP – transmission control protocol/internet protocol; layered set of protocols for networks.

TFU - texture filtering unit

Thread – smallest independent set of instructions managed by a multiprocessing operating system.

TLB – translation lookaside buffer – a cache of addresses.

Transceiver – receiver and transmitter in one box.

TRAP – exception or fault handling mechanism in a computer; an operating system component.

Triplicate – using three copies (of hardware, software, messaging, power supplies, etc.). for redundancy and error control.

Truncate – discard. Cutoff, make shorter.

TTL – transistor-transistor logic in digital integrated circuits. (1963)

UART – universal asynchronous receiver-transmitter. Parallel-to-serial; serial-to parallel device with handshaking.

UDP – User datagram protocol; part of the Internet Protocol.

USART – universal synchronous (or) asynchronous receiver/transmitter.

Underflow – the result of an arithmetic operation is smaller than the smallest representable number.

USB – universal serial bus.

Unsigned number – a number without a numeric sign.

Vector – single dimensional array of values.

VHDL- very high level description language; a language to describe integrated circuits and asic/ fpga's.

VIA – vertical conducting pathway through an insulating layer in a semiconductor.

Virtual memory – memory management technique using address translation.

Virtualization – creating a virtual resource from available physical resources.

Virus – malignant computer program.

VLIW – very long instruction word – mechanism for parallelism.

von Neumann – John, a computer pioneer and mathematician; realized that computer instructions are data.

Watchdog – hardware/software function to sanity check the hardware, software, and process; applies corrective action if a fault is detected; fail-safe mechanism.

Wiki – the Hawaiian word for "quick." Refers to a collaborative content website.

VLIW – very long instruction word.

Word – a collection of bits of any size; does not have to be a power of two.

Write-back – cache organization where the data is not written to main memory until the cache location is needed for re-use.

Write-only – of no interest.

Write-through – all cache writes also go to memory.

X86 – Intel 16-, 32-, 64-bit ISA.

XOR – exclusive OR; either but not both

Selected Bibliography

Abdallah, Ali E. *Communicating Sequential Processes. The First 25 Years: Symposium on the Occasion of 25 Years of CSP*, London, UK, July 7-8, 2004, Springer; 2005 edition ISBN-: 3540258132.

Abderazek, Ben Abadallah *Multicore Systems-on-chip: Practical Hardware/Software Design Issues (Atlantis Ambient and Pervasive Intelligence),* Atlantis Press, 2010, ISBN-10: 907867722.

Akhar, S. *Multi-Core Programming*, BPB Publications, 2010, ISBN-10: 8183333923.

ARM, Ltd. ARM11 MPCore Processor, Rev. r2p0, Technical Reference Manual, ARM, 2008.

Bakkers, A. Parallel Programming and Java: Wotug 20 : Proceedings of the 20th World Occam and Transputer User Group Technical Meeting, 13-16 April 1997 (Concurrent Systems Engineering Series, 50), Perfect Paperback, Ios Pr Inc.,October 1997, ISBN-9051993366.

Balasubramonian, Rajeev; Jouppi, Norman *Multi-Core Cache Hierarchies* (Synthesis Lectures on Computer Architecture) Morgan & Claypool Publishers; 1st edition, 2011, ISBN-1598297538.

Bell, C. Gordon and Newell, Allen, *Computer Structures: Readings and Examples,* McGraw-Hill Inc., January 1, 1971, ISBN- 0070043574.

Ben Abdallah, Abderazek Multi core Systems On-Chip: Practical Software/Hardware Design, Atlantis Press; 2013 ed., ISBN-9491216910.

Blaauw, Gerrit A. and Brooks, Frederick P. Jr. *Computer Architecture, Concepts and Evolution,* 2 volumes, 1997, Addison-Wesley, ISBN 0-201-10557-8.

Circello, Joe "Rationale for Multicore Architecture in Auto Apps, FTF-AUY-F0166, Freescale, June 2011.

Diaz-Martin, J.; Gutiérrez, C.G. ; Rico-Gallego, J. "Issues on Building an MPI Cluster on Microblaze," 2010 International Conference on Reconfigurable Computing and FPGAs (ReConFig), pp 220-225, ISBN-978-0-7695-4314-7.

Dowsing, R. D. *Introduction to Concurrency Using Occam,* Chapman & Hall, May 1988, ISBN-0278000592.

Doyle, Richard "High Performance Spaceflight Computing (HPSC) Study Report, Executive Summary," Jet Propulsion Lab Oct. 22, 2012.

Espenshade, Jeremy; von Laszweski, Gregor "Towards Heterogeneous Cluster Computing," Rochester Institute of Technology.

Espenshade, Jeremy; von Laszweski, Gregor; Lukowiak, Marcin; Flexible Framework for Commodity FPGA Cluster Computing, Rochester Institute of Technology, Dept. of Computer Engineering.

Flautner, Krisztián; Uhlig, Rich; Reinhardt, Steve; Mudge, Trevor; "Thread-level Parallelism and Interactive Performance of Desktop Applications," Aug. 21, 2000, University of Michigan, Intel Microprocessor Research Lab; in, Thread level parallelism and Interactive Performance of Desktop Applications - ASPLOS 2000.

Flynn, Michael J. *Computer Architecture: Pipelined and Parallel Processor Design,* 1995, Jones & Bartlett Learning; 1st ed, ISBN-0867202041.

Giorgi, Roberto (ed) *Multi-core and Many-core Computers: Dataflow Parallelism in Teradevice Computing,* Springer; 2012 ed, ISBN-10: 1461414830.

Gross, Thomas; Bell, Gordon; Kung, H.T. *iWARP: Anatomy of a Parallel Computing System,* The MIT Press (March 20, 1998) ISBN-0262071835 .

Hennessy, John L. and Patterson, David A. *Computer Architecture, Fifth Edition: A Quantitative Approach,* Morgan Kaufmann; (September 30, 2011) ISBN 012383872X.

Herlihy, Maurice; Nir Shavit, Nir *The Art of Multiprocessor Programming,* Morgan Kaufmann; 1st edition 2012, ISBN-10: 0123973376.

Hoare, C. A. R. (Ed) *Occam 2 Reference Manual* Inmos Limited (Prentice-Hall International Series in Computer Science), 1988, Prentice Hall, ISBN-0136293123.

Huerta, P.; J. Castillo, J.; Martinez, J. I.; Lopez A, V. *MicroBlaze Based Multiprocessor SoC,* Universidad Rey Juan Carlos, *Madrid, Spain.*

Inmos, *Occam Programming Manual*, Prentice Hall Trade, January 1984, ISBN-10: 0136292968.

Intel, http://goparallel.sourceforge.net/

Johnson, William M. *Superscalar Microprocessors Design*, Prentice Hall PTR; Facsimile edition (December 11, 1990) ISBN 0138756341.

Keckler, Stephen W. (Ed), Olukotun, Kunle (Ed), Hofstee, H. Peter (Ed) *Multicore Processors and Systems* (Integrated Circuits and Systems), Springer; 2009 edition, ISBN-10: 1441902627.

Keller, Rainer (Ed), Kramer, David (Ed), Weiss, Jan-Philipp (Ed) *Facing the Multicore-Challenge III: Aspects of New Paradigms and Technologies in Parallel Computing* (Lecture Notes in Computer Science / Theoretical Computer Science and General Issues) Springer; 2013 edition , ISBN-10: 3642358926.

Kornaros, Georgios *Multi-Core Embedded Systems,* CRC Press; 1st edition, 2010, ISBN-10: 143981161X.

Kowalczyk, Jeremy "Multiprocessor Systems," Xilinx White Paper WP162, April 10, 2003.

Ly, Daniel L.; Saldana, Manuel; Chow, Paul, The Challenges of Using An Embedded MPI for Hardware-based Processing Nodes, Dept. of electrical and computer Engineering, University of Toronto.

Mano, M. Morris *Computer System Architecture* (3rd Edition), Prentice Hall; 3rd edition (October 29, 1992) ISBN 0131755633.

Manoj Franklin, Zahran, Mohamed *Single-Chip Parallel Processing: The Era of Multicores and Manycores,* Morgan Kaufmann, 2011, ISBN-10: 0123744970.

Moyer. Bryon (ed) *Real World Multicore Embedded Systems*, Newnes; 1st edition, 2013, ISBN-10: 0124160182.

Murdocca, Miles J. and Heuring, Vincent *Computer Architecture and Organization: An Integrated Approach*, Wiley (March 16, 2007) ISBN 0471733881.

Nisan, Noam and Schocken, Shimon, *The Elements of Computing Systems: Building a Modern Computer from First Principles*, 2005, MIT Press, ISBN 0262640686.

Nosrati, Masoud; Karimi, Ronak "Occam: A Primary parallel programming language," World Applied

Programming, Vol. 1, No. 1, April 2011, pp85-88. ISSN 2222-2510. www.waprogramming.com

Null, Linda *The Essentials of Computer Organization And Architecture*, Jones & Bartlett Pub; 2 edition (February 15, 2006) ISBN 0763737690.

nVidia, Nvidia Kepler *GK110 Next-Generation CUDA Computer Architecture* Data sheet, 2012.

nVidia, *nVidia's Next Generation CUDA Compute Architecture*, Kepler GK110, White Paper, 2012.

nVidia, *Parallel thread Execution ISA, Application Guide*, v3.2 July 2013.

nVidia, Dynamic Parallelism in Cuda, 2012, nvidia.com

Olukotun, Kunle *Chip Multiprocessor Architecture: Techniques to Improve Throughput and Latency (Synthesis Lectures on Computer Architecture,)* Morgan and Claypool Publishers; 1st edition, 2007, ISBN-159829122X.

Padua, David (Ed) *Encyclopedia of Parallel Computing,* Springer; 2011 edition, ISBN-10: 0387097651.

Pankratius, Victor (Ed), Adl-Tabatabai, Ali-Reza (Ed), Tichy, Walter (Ed) *Fundamentals of Multicore Software Development*, CRC Press; 1st edition, 2011, ISBN-10: 143981273X.

Parallex (Co.) *Programming and Customizing the Multicore Propeller Microcontroller: The Official Guide* McGraw-Hill/TAB Electronics; 1st ed, 2010, ISBN-0071664505.

Patterson, David A and Hennessy, John L. *Computer Organization and Design: The Hardware/Software Interface*, Revised Fourth Edition, Morgan Kaufmann; Nov. 2011 ISBN 0123744938.

Pountain, D. May, David *Tutorial Introduction to Occam Programming* Alfred Waller Ltd, 1987, ISBN-063201847X .

Qadri, Muhammad Yasir (Ed), Sangwine, Stephen J. (Ed) *Multicore Technology: Architecture, Reconfiguration, and Modeling* (Embedded Multi-Core Systems), CRC Press; 1st edition, 2013, ISBN-10: 1439880638.

Quinn Michael J, *Parallel Programming in C with MPI and OpenMP* McGraw-Hill Inc. 2004. ISBN 0-07-058201-7

Rauber, Thomas Rünger Gudula *Parallel Programming: for Multicore and Cluster Systems,* Springer; 2010 ed., ISBN-10: 364204817X.

Reid, T. R. *The Chip: How Two Americans Invented the Microchip and Launched a Revolution*, Random House Trade Paperbacks; Revised edition (October 9, 2001) ISBN 0375758283.

Shriver, Bruce D. *The Anatomy of a High-Performance Microprocessor: A Systems Perspective*, Wiley-IEEE Computer Society Press (June 4, 1998) ISBN 0818684003.

Silc, Jurji; Robic, Borut; Ungerer, Theo; *Processor Architecture: From Dataflow to Superscalar and Beyond*, Springer; 1 edition (July 20, 1999) ISBN 3540647988.

Sorin, Daniel J.; Hill, Mark D.; Wood, David A. *A Primer on Memory Consistency and Cache Coherence* (Synthesis Lectures on Computer Architecture), Morgan & Claypool Publishers; 1st edition, 2012, ISBN-10: 1608455645.

Stakem, Patrick H. *The Architecture and Applications of the ARM Microprocessors,* PRRB Publishing, Feb 2013, B00BAFF4OQ.

Stakem, Patrick H. *Computer Architecture & Programming of the Intel x86 Family,* 1988, PRRB Publishing, ASIN B0078Q39D4, ISBN 0972596657.

Stakem, Patrick H. *Architecture of Massively Parallel Microprocessor Systems*, PRRB Publishing, Jan, 2011, ASIN: B004K1F172, ISBN 097259664X.

Stakem, Patrick H. *Floating Point Computation,* 2013, PRRB Publishing, ASIN B00D5E1S7W.

Stakem, Patrick H. *The Hardware and Software Architecture of the Transputer*, 2011, PRRB Publishing, ASIN B004OYTS1K.

Stakem, Patrick H. *A Practitioner's guide to RISC Microprocessor Architecture, 1996, Wiley-Interscience,* ISBN 978-0471130185.

Stakem, Patrick H. *Embedded Computer Systems, Volume 1, Introduction and Architecture,2013, PRRB Publishing,* ASIN B00GB0W4GG.

Stallings, William *Computer Organization and Architecture: Designing for Performance* (7th Edition), Prentice Hall; 7 edition (July 21, 2005) ISBN 0131856448.

Stokes, Jon, *Inside the Machine An Illustrated Introduction to Microprocessors and Computer Architecture*, 2006, No Starch Press, ISBN 1593271042.

Texas Instruments, Multicore Fact Sheet, 2010. www.ti.com

Unified Parallel C - UPC Specifications, LBNL-59208,

http://www.gwu.edu/~upc/publications/ibm05.pdf

Van Someren, Alex and Atack, Carol, *ARM RISC Chip: A Programmer's Guide*, 1994, Addison Wesley, ISBN 0201624109.

wikipedia, various.

Xilinx MicroBlaze Processor Reference Guide, June 2006, www.xilinx.com

Tanaka, Kazuto, et al "The Design and Performance of SpaceWire Router-network using CSP," 2008, avail: http://citeseerx.ist.psu.edu/viewdoc/summary? doi=10.1.1.695.538.

Sputh, Bernard H. C., et al "Portable CSP Based Design for Embedded Multi-Core Systems, In Communicating Process Architectures, 2006, IOS Press.

Manjunathaiah, M. "CSP as a general Concurrency Model," (Powerpoint), PoPP11-WCPath, Feb 1, 2011, San Antonio, TX, avail: engineering.perdue.edu

Vinter, Brian "Old Tricks for New Architectures: Teaching CSP ofr Multi-core Programming," avail:

https://www.researchgate.net/publication/237355365_Old_Tricks_for_New_Architectures_Teaching_CSP_for_Multi-core_Programming

If you enjoyed this book, you might also be interested in some of these.

Stakem, Patrick H. *16-bit Microprocessors, History and Architecture*, 2013 PRRB Publishing, ISBN-1520210922.

Stakem, Patrick H. *4- and 8-bit Microprocessors, Architecture and History*, 2013, PRRB Publishing, ISBN-152021572X,

Stakem, Patrick H. *Apollo's Computers,* 2014, PRRB Publishing, ISBN-1520215800.

Stakem, Patrick H. *The Architecture and Applications of the ARM Microprocessors,* 2013, PRRB Publishing, ISBN-1520215843.

Stakem, Patrick H. *Earth Rovers: for Exploration and Environmental Monitoring,* 2014, PRRB Publishing, ISBN-152021586X.

Stakem, Patrick H. *Embedded Computer Systems, Volume 1, Introduction and Architecture*, 2013, PRRB Publishing, ISBN-1520215959.

Stakem, Patrick H. *The History of Spacecraft Computers from the V-2 to the Space Station*, 2013, PRRB Publishing, ISBN-1520216181.

Stakem, Patrick H. *Floating Point Computation*, 2013, PRRB Publishing, ISBN-152021619X.

Stakem, Patrick H. *Architecture of Massively Parallel Microprocessor Systems*, 2011, PRRB Publishing, ISBN-1520250061.

Stakem, Patrick H. *Multicore Computer Architecture,* 2014, PRRB Publishing, ISBN-1520241372.

Stakem, Patrick H. *Personal Robots*, 2014, PRRB Publishing, ISBN-1520216254.

Stakem, Patrick H. *RISC Microprocessors, History and Overview,* 2013, PRRB Publishing, ISBN-1520216289.

Stakem, Patrick H. *Robots and Telerobots in Space Applications*, 2011, PRRB Publishing, ISBN-1520210361.

Stakem, Patrick H. *The Saturn Rocket and the Pegasus Missions, 1965,* 2013, PRRB Publishing, ISBN-1520209916.

Stakem, Patrick H. *Visiting the NASA Centers, and Locations of Historic Rockets & Spacecraft,* 2017, PRRB Publishing, ISBN-1549651205.

Stakem, Patrick H. *Microprocessors in Space*, 2011, PRRB Publishing, ISBN-1520216343.

Stakem, Patrick H. Computer *Virtualization and the Cloud*, 2013, PRRB Publishing, ISBN-152021636X.

Stakem, Patrick H. *What's the Worst That Could Happen? Bad Assumptions, Ignorance, Failures and Screw-ups in Engineering Projects, 2014,* PRRB Publishing, ISBN-1520207166.

Stakem, Patrick H. *Computer Architecture & Programming of the Intel x86 Family, 2013,* PRRB Publishing, ISBN-1520263724.

Stakem, Patrick H. *The Hardware and Software Architecture of the Transputer*, 2011,PRRB Publishing, ISBN-152020681X.

Stakem, Patrick H. *Mainframes, Computing on Big Iron*, 2015, PRRB Publishing, ISBN- 1520216459.

Stakem, Patrick H. *Spacecraft Control Centers*, 2015, PRRB Publishing, ISBN-1520200617.

Stakem, Patrick H. *Embedded in Space,* 2015, PRRB Publishing, ISBN-1520215916.

Stakem, Patrick H. *A Practitioner's Guide to RISC Microprocessor Architecture*, Wiley-Interscience, 1996, ISBN-0471130184.

Stakem, Patrick H. *Cubesat Engineering*, PRRB Publishing, 2017, ISBN-1520754019.

Stakem, Patrick H. *Cubesat Operations*, PRRB Publishing, 2017, ISBN-152076717X.

Stakem, Patrick H. *Interplanetary Cubesats*, PRRB Publishing, 2017, ISBN-1520766173 .

Stakem, Patrick H. Cubesat Constellations, Clusters, and Swarms, Stakem, PRRB Publishing, 2017, ISBN-1520767544.

Stakem, Patrick H. *Graphics Processing Units, an overview*, 2017, PRRB Publishing, ISBN-1520879695.

Stakem, Patrick H. *Intel Embedded and the Arduino-101, 2017,* PRRB Publishing, ISBN-1520879296.

Stakem, Patrick H. *Orbital Debris, the problem and the mitigation*, 2018, PRRB Publishing, ISBN-*1980466483.*

Stakem, Patrick H. *Manufacturing in Space*, 2018, PRRB Publishing, ISBN-1977076041.

Stakem, Patrick H. *NASA's Ships and Planes*, 2018, PRRB Publishing, ISBN-1977076823.

Stakem, Patrick H. *Space Tourism*, 2018, PRRB Publishing, ISBN-1977073506.

Stakem, Patrick H. *STEM – Data Storage and Communications*, 2018, PRRB Publishing, ISBN-1977073115.

Stakem, Patrick H. *In-Space Robotic Repair and Servicing*, 2018, PRRB Publishing, ISBN-1980478236.

Stakem, Patrick H. *Introducing Weather in the pre-K to 12 Curricula, A Resource Guide for Educators*, 2017, PRRB Publishing, ISBN-1980638241.

Stakem, Patrick H. *Introducing Astronomy in the pre-K to 12 Curricula, A Resource Guide for Educators*, 2017, PRRB Publishing, ISBN-198104065X.

Also available in a Brazilian Portuguese edition, ISBN-1983106127.

Stakem, Patrick H. *Deep Space Gateways, the Moon and Beyond*, 2017, PRRB Publishing, ISBN-1973465701.

Stakem, Patrick H. *Exploration of the Gas Giants, Space Missions to Jupiter, Saturn, Uranus, and Neptune*, PRRB Publishing, 2018, ISBN-9781717814500.

Stakem, Patrick H. *Crewed Spacecraft*, 2017, PRRB Publishing, ISBN-1549992406.

Stakem, Patrick H. *Rocketplanes to Space*, 2017, PRRB Publishing, ISBN-1549992589.

Stakem, Patrick H. *Crewed Space Stations,* 2017, PRRB Publishing, ISBN-1549992228.

Stakem, Patrick H. *Enviro-bots for STEM: Using Robotics in the pre-K to 12 Curricula, A Resource Guide for Educators,* 2017, PRRB Publishing, ISBN-1549656619.

Stakem, Patrick H. *STEM-Sat, Using Cubesats in the pre-K to 12 Curricula, A Resource Guide for Educators*, 2017, ISBN-1549656376.

Stakem, Patrick H. *Lunar Orbital Platform-Gateway*, 2018, PRRB Publishing, ISBN-1980498628.

Stakem, Patrick H. *Embedded GPU's*, 2018, PRRB Publishing, ISBN- 1980476497.

Stakem, Patrick H. *Mobile Cloud Robotics*, 2018, PRRB Publishing, ISBN- 1980488088.

Stakem, Patrick H. *Extreme Environment Embedded Systems,* 2017, PRRB Publishing, ISBN-1520215967.

Stakem, Patrick H. *What's the Worst, Volume-2*, 2018, ISBN-1981005579.

Stakem, Patrick H., *Spaceports*, 2018, ISBN-1981022287.

Stakem, Patrick H., *Space Launch Vehicles*, 2018, ISBN-1983071773.

Stakem, Patrick H. *Mars*, 2018, ISBN-1983116902.

Stakem, Patrick H. *X-86, 40th Anniversary ed*, 2018, ISBN-1983189405.

Stakem, Patrick H. *Lunar Orbital Platform-Gateway*, 2018, PRRB Publishing, ISBN-1980498628.

Stakem, Patrick H. *Space Weather*, 2018, ISBN-1723904023.

Stakem, Patrick H. *STEM-Engineering Process*, 2017, ISBN-1983196517.

Stakem, Patrick H. *Space Telescopes,* 2018, PRRB Publishing, ISBN-1728728568.

Stakem, Patrick H. *Exoplanets*, 2018, PRRB Publishing, ISBN-9781731385055.

Stakem, Patrick H. *Planetary Defense*, 2018, PRRB Publishing, ISBN-9781731001207.

Patrick H. Stakem *Exploration of the Asteroid Belt*, 2018, PRRB Publishing, ISBN-1731049846.

Patrick H. Stakem *Terraforming*, 2018, PRRB Publishing, ISBN-1790308100.

Patrick H. Stakem, *Martian Railroad,* 2019, PRRB Publishing, ISBN-1794488243.

Patrick H. Stakem, *Exoplanets,* 2019, PRRB Publishing, ISBN-1731385056.

Patrick H. Stakem, *Exploiting the Moon,* 2019, PRRB Publishing, ISBN-1091057850.

Patrick H. Stakem, *RISC-V, an Open Source Solution for Space Flight Computers,* 2019, PRRB Publishing, ISBN-1796434388.

Patrick H. Stakem, *Arm in Space*, 2019, PRRB Publishing, ISBN-9781099789137.

Patrick H. Stakem, *Extraterrestrial Life*, 2019, PRRB Publishing, ISBN-978-1072072188.

Patrick H. Stakem, *Space Command*, 2019, PRRB Publishing, ISBN-978-1693005398.

CubeRovers, A Synergy of Technologys, 2020, PRRB Publishing, ISBN-979-8651773138.

Robotic Exploration of the Icy moons of the Gas Giants. 2020, PRRB Publishing, ISBN- 979-8621431006

Hacking Cubesats, 2020, PRRB Publishing, ISBN-979-8623458964.

History & Future of Cubesats, PRRB Publishing, ISBN-979-8649179386.

Hacking Cubesats, Cybersecurity in Space, 2020, PRRB Publishing, ISBN-979-8623458964.

Powerships, Powerbarges, Floating Wind Farms: electricity when and where you need it, 2021, PRRB Publishing, ISBN-979-8716199477.

Hospital Ships, Trains, and Aircraft, 2020, PRRB Publishing, ISBN-979-8642944349.

2020/2021 Releases

CubeRovers, a Synergy of Technologys, 2020, ISBN-979-8651773138

Exploration of Lunar & Martian Lava Tubes by Cube-X, ISBN-979-8621435325.

Robotic Exploration of the Icy moons of the Gas Giants, ISBN- 979-8621431006.

History & Future of Cubesats, ISBN-978-1986536356.

Robotic Exploration of the Icy Moons of the Ice Giants, by Swarms of Cubesats, ISBN-979-8621431006.

Swarm Robotics, ISBN-979-8534505948.

Introduction to Electric Power Systems, ISBN-979-8519208727.

Centros de Control: Operaciones en Satélites del Estándar CubeSat (Spanish Edition), 2021, ISBN-979-8510113068.

Exploration of Venus, 2022, ISBN-979-8484416110.

Patrick H. Stakem, *The Search for Extraterrestial Life*, 2019, PRRB Publishing, ISBN-1072072181.

The Artemis Missions, Return to the Moon, and on to Mars, 2021, ISBN-979-8490532361.

James Webb Space Telescope. A New Era in Astronomy, 2021, ISBN-979-8773857969.

Riverine Ironclads, Submarines, and Aircraft Carriers of the American Civil War, 2019, ISBN- 978-1089379287.